A GOOD MAN

A Comedy in Two Acts

by Frederick Stroppel

SAMUEL FRENCH, INC.

45 West 25th Street   NEW YORK 10010
7623 Sunset Boulevard HOLLYWOOD 90046
LONDON   TORONTO

IMPORTANT BILLING AND CREDIT REQUIREMENTS

All producers of A GOOD MAN *must* give credit to the Author of the Play in all programs distributed in connection with performances of the Play and in all instances in which the title of the Play appears for purposes of advertising, publicizing or otherwise exploiting the Play and/or a production. The name of the Author *must* also appear on a separate line, on which no other name appears, immediately following the title, and *must* appear in size of type not less than fifty percent the size of the title type.

A *Good Man* was first presented by the Courtyard Players on April 27, 1988, at the Courtyard Playhouse in New York City. The cast was as follows:

JIMMY LAMB ....Rob Tossberg
MARTIN LAMB............................Joseph Callari
SHARON MULDOON ....Melissa Yade
DOUGLAS PORTEUS ....Charles Moore
ANDREW PORTEUS ....Donald Viscardi
GLORIA PORTEUS ....Denize Kazan
BOBBY GELARDI.........................Bob Wilkens
NORMA CZERNIAWSKI ......Mary Jane Keehn
YOLANDA KAMOLA ....Mina Apovian

Directed by ....Kevin O'Connor
Assistant Director................Debbon Ayer Lutken
Stage Manager ....Amy Whitman
Set and Lighting Designer ....Larry Springer
Costume Designer.......................Sue Jane Stoker
Sound Designer ....Franklin Micare
Production Manager ....David Mead
Executive Producer ....Melissa Yade

CHARACTERS

MARTIN LAMB, the funeral director

JIMMY LAMB, apprentice to his father

MR. WALTER PORTEUS, the deceased

SHARON MULDOON, daughter of the deceased

DOUGLAS PORTEUS, elder son of the deceased

GLORIA PORTEUS, wife to the elder son

ANDREW PORTEUS, younger son of the deceased

BOBBY GELARDI, air-conditioning and refrigeration specialist

NORMA CZERNIAWSKI, a visitor

YOLANDA KAMOLA, young lady with clear complexion

MR. CAMPBELL, deceased in a cameo role

TIME & PLACE

The action takes place in the beautiful Lilac
Room of the Good Shepherd Funeral Parlor.

ACT I
Scene 1: A hot July afternoon, around 2:30
Scene 2: That evening, 8:45 p.m.

ACT II
Scene 1: A few seconds after the end of Act I
Scene 2: The next morning

A GOOD MAN

ACT I
Scene 1

The Lilac Room of the Good Shepherd Funeral Parlor. The room, appropriately painted in a lilac shade, has one entrance, two large paneled doors which lead to an outer lobby, stage left of center. Far stage left is another smaller door, which leads to an office. Stage right there is a window.

The room is furnished with a few armchairs and a small couch against the walls, and a number of folding chairs in the middle of the room. There are also unopened folding chairs off to the side. Stage left by the large door there is a stand with a register book atop it. There are also several lamp tables. Upstage center is an open casket, containing a BODY. The casket is flanked with a few floral tributes—a rather small display. A floral blanket, bearing the word "DAD" is spread over the lower half of the casket.

A YOUNG MAN kneels before the casket, head bowed, seemingly deep in prayer. HIS body shudders silently, as if weeping. After a moment, as HE turns slightly, HE is revealed to be actually polishing the side of the casket with a chamois cloth. HE pauses and peers carefully at the wood. HE glances about, and then surreptitiously spits on the wood. HE polishes the spot.

Rising to his feet, the casket cleaner, JIMMY LAMB, in his early twenties, runs the cloth along the top edging of

the casket. With great casualness HE reaches in to quickly dust the body. HE steps back to admire his work.
After a moment, JIMMY spins away, does a pirouette, and executes a perfect jump shot, tossing the cloth as if it were a basketball. The cloth lands in the casket.

JIMMY. (*Punching the air with his fist.*) Yes! (*JIMMY retrieves the cloth, and tries a shot from another angle. The cloth falls short.*) Blocks the shot ... Rebound ...

(*JIMMY scoops up the cloth and races downstage. The office door opens, and MARTIN LAMB, the funeral director, enters. HE is a man in his early fifties, impeccably dressed in a suitably solemn fashion. HE stops short, and watches his son.*
JIMMY, unaware of Lamb, turns and charges the casket. HE slam-dunks the cloth into the casket.)

JIMMY. In your face!

(*JIMMY raises his hands to acknowledge the cheers. HE turns and sees his father. HE immediately lowers his arms and clears his throat, attempting to assume a serious demeanor. As LAMB stares at him disapprovingly, JIMMY retrieves the cloth.*)

LAMB. You didn't muss his make-up, did you?
JIMMY. I don't think so. (*Pointing.*) Is that supposed to be there?
LAMB. (*Looking into the casket.*) Yes, that's scar tissue.

Childhood accident, I believe.

JIMMY. Couldn't cover it up?

LAMB. (*Indignant.*) I can cover *anything* up. I chose *not* to cover it up; it was an aesthetic choice. I find that this particular scar lends Mr. Porteus here a certain dash, a panache; or, if you will, a je ne sais quois.

JIMMY. (*Regarding his face.*) He was an ugly son-of-a-bitch.

LAMB. (*Disapproving.*) James ...

JIMMY. What's the difference? He's dead now.

LAMB. How many times must I tell you, you have to resist the temptation to make sport of our customers? It's not professional. Besides, his soul may be sitting on your shoulder.

JIMMY. I'm sorry, Dad. I guess I'm just not sensitive enough for this business.

LAMB. Nonsense, you're doing fine. No one's a born mortician. It takes time and experience. (*HE takes his jacket off.*) Lord, this heat ... Do me a favor, see what that electrician is up to. If we don't get this air-conditioning fixed soon, we're going to have a problem with spoilage.

(*JIMMY exits through the doors into the lobby. LAMB wipes his face with a handkerchief. HE leans against the casket and resumes speaking, apparently to Mr. Porteus.*)

LAMB. Modern technology. In the old days we'd have those tall standing fans in the corner. Cooled off the whole room at a fraction of the cost. Kept the flies moving, too. (*HE looks into the casket.*)You *are* an ugly son-of-a-bitch, there's no doubt about it. Sloping forehead, prognathic jaw, asymmetrical distribution of the eyes ... But don't let it bother you; it's of no consequence now. You might have to suffer through one day of public display, but tomorrow we'll have a nice funeral for you, and you can leave that face behind forever. Pursue a sublimely incorporeal existence, and seduce the angels ... (*With some disappointment.*) I wish I could have done something about that smile. It just won't sit right.

(*HE reaches in and pokes at the face a little. JIMMY returns.*)

JIMMY. The family's here.

LAMB. (*Looks at his watch; irritated.*) I told them two-thirty. They always come early. I don't know what the rush is.

JIMMY. Should I let them in?

LAMB No, let them wait. It'll put them in a more reverent frame of mind. What did the electrician say?

JIMMY. He says he's not an electrician, he's an air-conditioning-and-refrigeration specialist. And he's going to lunch.

LAMB. That's fine. Everyone's so independent these days. They forget that someday they're going to need me. And maybe I'll just let them rot. (*LAMB moves about the room, setting everything in order.*)

JIMMY. Dad, are you going to want me here tonight?

LAMB. Want you? Certainly. We'll have Mr. Porteus in here, and Mrs. Hartigan in the Daffodil Room, and Mr. Campbell in the Rose Room. Mr. Campbell was an Elk, and a Volunteer Fireman, so you know what a mob scene that's going to be. Why, do you have plans?

JIMMY. It *is* Friday night. I'm supposed to meet a friend.

LAMB. (*Carefully stacking the memorial cards beside the register book.*) We'll be finished by 9:30.

JIMMY. But she lives out in Commack. That's almost an hour's ride.

LAMB. (*With fatherly concern.*) She?

JIMMY. Yes, she's sort of a girl.

LAMB. Does she have a name?

JIMMY. Yolanda.

LAMB. (*Thoughtfully.*) Yolanda ... We had a woman here last February whose name was Yolanda. She had a distressing amount of body hair. I'm not suggesting that this is typical, mind you, but I will admit that it came as no surprise to me.

JIMMY. (*With great fervor.*) My Yolanda is the most hairless of women. Her skin is smooth and creamy, and it glows from some inner source of radiance. She's made of butter and sunshine, and she's so fresh, so wholesome, so American. What little hair she has is like an oasis on a golden desert, the long silken tendrils flowering in a lush velvet undergrowth. (*LAMB looks at him quizzically.*) And she has a very pleasant disposition.

LAMB. Yes, when you're composed of various dairy products, I suppose that comes naturally. I'd like very much to meet this Yolanda.

JIMMY. Well ... She's extremely shy.

LAMB That doesn't matter. You know that I excel in defusing awkward situations. Why don't you have her meet you here? I can give her a tour of the facility.

JIMMY. No, that wouldn't be a good idea.

LAMB. Why not? Most lay people are fascinated by the

workings of a state-of-the-art mortuary. And there's no one in the embalming room tonight—you know, if you want to be alone ...

JIMMY. I'm not sure she can handle it ...

LAMB. Handle what?

(There is a light KNOCK on the door. LAMB is irritated.)

LAMB. These people have no patience. Are they afraid they're going to miss something? (*LAMB puts on his jacket.*) Well, I'd like to help you, Jimmy, but I'm really going to need you tonight. You know, that's the nature of this business: sacrifice. The show must go on. I know it seems hard now, but someday, when all this is yours, you'll be glad your old man instilled you with a proper sense of priorities.

JIMMY. Well, Dad, that's something else I wanted to talk to you about ...

LAMB How do I look? (*HE straightens out Jimmy's jacket, picks lint off his shoulder.*) Where's your flower?

(JIMMY walks over to a floral wreath and picks off a flower.
LAMB takes a small notebook from his pocket.)

LAMB. Mr. Walter Porteus, seventy-two years old, expired from a massive heart attack, brought on by a ruptured aorta ... (*Looking down on Mr. Porteus sympathetically.*) That'll do it. (*Consulting the book.*) Owner of the Porteus Pharmacy in Glen Head for the past thirty-six years ... Wife deceased, three children living ... The eldest son is named Douglas, he owns his own business, and he's married to a woman from Queens ...

JIMMY. I saw her. She looks hot.

LAMB. (*Glances at Jimmy, shakes his head, and returns to his notebook.*) The younger son, Andrew, is unmarried and unemployed. And the daughter, Sharon, is divorced. No children, thank God. (*HE puts away the notebook.*) So ... Take a deep breath ... (*THEY take deep breaths.*) Keep the shoulders back ... Speak in soft, modulated tones. Eschew all morbid discourse. And watch out for fainters. It's ...

LAMB & JIMMY. (*Together.*) ... always the person you least expect.

(*LAMB smiles proudly, and directs Jimmy to the door. HE walks over to the casket, and gives the body the once-over.*)

LAMB. Well, Mr. Porteus, this is it. Your children are waiting to see you, and soon your friends will be here, and it will be just one big party. And don't you look nice for them! (*HE pokes at the face.*) Except that smile. (*LAMB steps away from the casket, clears his throat, and mentally prepares himself. HE signals to Jimmy at the door.*) It's magic time!

(*JIMMY opens the doors wide, and beckons.*
The PORTEUS FAMILY enters the room.
Leading the group is SHARON MULDOON. In her late thirties, SHE wears a dark grey dress, and is somewhat weepy; SHE holds a handkerchief at the ready.
DOUGLAS PORTEUS, a year older, follows. HE is tall, imposing, and not at all pleased at having to attend his

father's wake on a business day.
ANDREW PORTEUS, bringing up the rear, is about
*   thirty-five. HE wears a suit that is ill-fitting and*
*   unpressed.*
As THEY slowly make their way into the room, LAMB
*   approaches solemnly. Coming near to Sharon, HE*
*   breaks into a most sympathetic smile.)*

LAMB. *(Taking Sharon's hand.)* He was a good man.

(SHARON bursts into tears.
LAMB guides her to a folding chair, where SHE sits and
*   weeps.*
LAMB turns to Douglas and shakes his hand.)

LAMB. Mr. Porteus. So good of you to come.
DOUGLAS. I can't see that I had much choice. Jesus,
it's hot in here.
LAMB. The air-conditioning is temporarily down.
DOUGLAS. I don't suppose we can expect a discount?

(LAMB smiles politely, assuming this to be a joke. HE
*   moves on to Andrew.*
ANDREW has picked up the stack of memorial cards. HE
*   quickly rifles through them, and realizes that they're all*
*   the same. Absently HE shuffles them.)*

LAMB. Mr. Porteus ...?

(ANDREW turns quickly and shakes LAMB's hand with
*   exuberance. HE has a habit of talking a little too loud*
*   and a little too fast.)*

ANDREW. Hi! How are you?
LAMB. (*Taken aback.*) Uh ... I'm fine.
ANDREW. (*Holding up a memorial card.*) Hey, look. Saint Francis. My favorite.
LAMB. (*Disconcerted, HE forges ahead.*) Allow me to offer my deepest condolences on this very sad occasion ...

(*LAMB trails off, watching aghast as ANDREW scrapes his shoe against the rug, trying to dislodge a substance from the sole.*)

ANDREW. (*Looks down at the rug, and smiles.*) It's only gum. (*To Lamb.*) So, what, you own this place?
DOUGLAS. That's a brilliant question. What does he look like, the janitor?
ANDREW. I wasn't talking to you.
DOUGLAS. So keep your voice down. This is a wake; show some fucking respect.
SHARON. (*Looking up from her handkerchief.*) What kind of language is that to use?
DOUGLAS. I wasn't talking to you.
ANDREW. *I* wasn't talking to *you!*

(*ANDREW and DOUGLAS glare at each other, while SHARON resumes weeping. LAMB sidles over to Jimmy.*)

LAMB. I sense a little family tension here. You'd better turn on the Muzak.

(*JIMMY nods, and exits.*

DOUGLAS turns to Lamb.)

DOUGLAS. Weren't we supposed to have the Lilac Room?

LAMB. This is the Lilac Room.

DOUGLAS. I thought the big room was the Lilac Room. I was here about seven months ago for Charlie DiMasso's wake ...

LAMB. Ah, Charlie DiMasso. He was a good man.

DOUGLAS. He was a good man, and he was in the Lilac Room.

LAMB. But that's the Rose Room now. And the old Rose Room is the Daffodil Room, and this is now the Lilac Room. We painted the walls, you see. Can't afford to stand pat in this business.

DOUGLAS. I have no argument with your decorating scheme. But my father would have wanted the big room.

LAMB. We had to give Mr. Campbell the Rose Room. He's an Elk.

DOUGLAS. Everything's politics. (*Looking towards the door.*) Where's Gloria?

SHARON. Maybe she's in the ladies' room.

ANDREW. (*To Sharon.*) Maybe she's in the men's room.

(*SHARON and ANDREW share a furtive laugh, and then SHARON resumes her mourning. ANDREW approaches Lamb.*)

ANDREW. Do you think we'll get a lot of quail here today?

LAMB. Quail ... ?

ANDREW. You know. Women.

LAMB. Oh. Quail. Yes, I'm sure both sexes will be well represented.

ANDREW. I don't get dressed up that often; I might as well take advantage of the opportunity ...

DOUGLAS. (*Coming away from the door.*) Gloria did get out of the car, didn't she? Maybe she went shopping. (*To Lamb.*) Are there any department stores in this neighborhood? My wife can usually smell a JC Penney's a mile away.

LAMB. No, mostly banks and restaurants. There's a bookstore on the corner.

ANDREW. Maybe she's buying a book. *(HE laughs at the idea.)*

DOUGLAS. (*Wheeling on Andrew.*) What do you mean by that? Are you saying that Gloria is stupid?

ANDREW. Uh ... Yeah.

DOUGLAS. (*Grabbing Andrew roughly.*) Why, you ...

ANDREW. (*Wriggling free.*) Hey! Don't wrinkle my jacket!

DOUGLAS. (*Threateningly.*) If we weren't in a funeral parlor I'd lay you out right now.

ANDREW. (*Taking refuge behind an armchair.*) I'm not afraid of you.

SHARON. (*Annoyed.*) Will you two stop it? I'm trying to mourn over here.

DOUGLAS. I told you we shouldn't have brought him.

SHARON. You can't keep him away from his own father's wake.

ANDREW. Yeah! I got my rights.

DOUGLAS. (*Walking away.*) A pain in the ass from the day he was born.

SHARON. (*Takes ANDREW aside.*) Andy, are you on something?

ANDREW. No. You know I don't do that stuff anymore.

SHARON. You were stoned yesterday when I called you.

ANDREW. Yeah, but that wasn't my stuff. Somebody gave it to me. What was I going to say, "No"?

SHARON. Your brother and I would both appreciate it if just this once you kept your head straight and didn't act like an idiot.

ANDREW. (*Offended.*) Like when?

SHARON. Like Ma's funeral. Like Grandpa's funeral. Like cousin Gail's wedding. Like last Easter Sunday. Like the PBA's "300 Club" Dinner. Like the Veteran's Day Parade.

ANDREW. Those were all isolated incidents.

SHARON. Please try to behave yourself. Remember, Dad's looking down on you. Make him proud.

ANDREW. (*Muttering to himself.*) I was a veteran, anyway. They were giving the fucking parade for me.

(*Soft MUSIC floats in over the Muzak. LAMB is visibly relieved.*)

LAMB. Would anyone like to view the Beloved?

(*There is an awkward pause.*)

DOUGLAS. Sharon, why don't you start it off? You're the daughter.

ANDREW. Yeah, go for it.

(SHARON, finding herself thus elected, turns towards the casket. SHE is about to weep when SHE realizes that SHE doesn't have her handkerchief. SHE picks it up off her chair, and cries into it as SHE approaches the casket. LAMB solicitously leads her along. Suddenly the PHONE rings offstage in the office. SHARON turns in annoyance, the mood of reverent grief having been rudely dispelled.
JIMMY enters from the lobby.
LAMB frantically signals to him to answer the phone.
JIMMY rushes into the office.
As the ringing ceases, SHARON resumes crying into her handkerchief as SHE approaches the casket. SHE kneels before the casket and bows her head. LAMB steps away and stands to the side, his hands respectfully folded. After a moment of silent prayer, SHARON suddenly rises and turns away from the casket. SHE is noticeably upset.)

SHARON. (*To Lamb.*) Where's his blue suit? He's not wearing his blue suit!

LAMB. That's the suit he came with.

SHARON. (*To Douglas.*) I told you, the *blue* suit. (*To Lamb.*) He left specific instructions that he wished to be buried in his navy blue Palm Beach suit.

DOUGLAS. I dropped it off yesterday. Why, what's he wearing?

SHARON. Tweed. He can't be buried in that. It's the wrong season.

LAMB. I'm sorry if there's been a mix-up, but we are very careful about dressing our people. If you'd like to bring down the suit in question, we can have him ready for the evening show ... uh, session.

DOUGLAS. (*Looking into the casket.*) You know, this is not only the wrong suit in the wrong season; this is the wrong body.

(*Astonished, the OTHERS approach the casket.
SHARON gasps in horror.*)

ANDREW. Yeah, that's not Dad.

LAMB. (*Dumfounded.*) You mean to say this isn't your father?

DOUGLAS. I don't recognize him.

LAMB. Are you sure? We were necessarily liberal in our use of cosmetics.

ANDREW. (*Thoughtfully.*) That could make a difference.

DOUGLAS. The only way this guy could be my father is if you applied his make-up with a sledgehammer.

SHARON. How could you put this ugly man in my father's suit?

ANDREW. At least it's not the blue suit.

LAMB. I don't know how this could have happened ... There may have been some confusion at the hospital. But this is the body that was delivered to us yesterday afternoon. I checked the toe-tag personally.

ANDREW. Maybe somebody switched the tags, as a joke.

SHARON. I don't see anything funny.in that.

ANDREW. (*Shrugging.*) I do.

LAMB. Your father *was* about this age?

SHARON. Yes ...

LAMB. The jacket seems to fit him. We didn't have to pad the shoulders.

SHARON. How tall is he?

LAMB. Five-eight.

DOUGLAS. My father was five-ten.

LAMB. With age you get a certain shrinkage.

SHARON. He has the same forehead ...

DOUGLAS. I don't care if he has the same dental work. He's the wrong guy. (*To Lamb.*) Now where do you suppose my father is? Downstairs in the refrigerator?

LAMB. No, we don't have any back-up today. He may have been sent to another funeral home.

SHARON. Oh, that's great.

DOUGLAS. I hope their prices are lower.

SHARON. (*Looking at her watch.*) And all our friends will be here any minute now.

LAMB. Maybe he's still at the hospital.

ANDREW. Maybe he's not even dead. Let me call home.

SHARON. Suppose he's been cremated? I didn't get a chance to kiss him goodbye.

LAMB. There's no need to panic. Perhaps my son can clear this matter up.

(*As LAMB starts towards the office, GLORIA PORTEUS, Douglas' wife, enters from the hallway. SHE is a very attractive woman, and SHE dresses to favor this sole asset. LAMB reflexively greets her as SHE enters.*)

LAMB. (*Shaking her hand.*) He was a good man ...

GLORIA. (*To Douglas.*) What's everyone doing in here?

DOUGLAS. We're having a cocktail party. Where were

you?

GLORIA. I was in the big room. (*Pointing to the casket.*) Who's that?

ANDREW. Dad couldn't make it. This is the understudy.

GLORIA. Your father's in the other room. And he looks *wonderful.*

DOUGLAS. (*To Lamb, as THEY move into the hall.*) I told you he wanted the big room.

(*LAMB and DOUGLAS exit into the hall.*)

ANDREW. Since this isn't even the right body, I'm taking my jacket off. (*HE tosses his jacket over a chair.*)

SHARON. (*Quite frazzled.*) Can you believe that? They don't even know who they're burying. Or maybe they thought we wouldn't notice.

GLORIA. That isn't right. You are paying top dollar, after all. (*SHE looks into the casket.*) Good Lord, what a face. The scar is kind of sexy, though.

SHARON. And I wasted a prayer on him, too. For all I know he's an atheist.

(*DOUGLAS and LAMB return.*)

DOUGLAS. That's him. He's in the Rose Room.

ANDREW. At least he didn't wander to far off.

LAMB. I can only assume that this is Mr. Campbell here.

DOUGLAS. He looks like an Elk.

LAMB. This is really an inexcusable error, and I take full responsibility. Now the simplest remedy would be to switch rooms. But I'm afraid that Mr. Campbell has a firm reservation on the Rose Room, and, the funeral business being what it is these days, I have no desire to invite litigation on such a minor point. (*To Douglas.*) Unless you would like to speak to his people?

DOUGLAS. (*Glancing at Mr. Campbell.*) I don't want to have anything to do with his people. Can't you just move Dad in here?

LAMB. Well, if it wouldn't be too offensive to family members ...

DOUGLAS. We just want to get *on* with it.

JIMMY. (*Enters from the office.*) Hey, Dad, there's a guy on the phone who wants to know if we bury animals ...

LAMB. (*Taking JIMMY aside.*) Never mind that. We've got a problem here. Scarface belongs in the Rose Room. We have to move him *now.* (*HE turns back to the family.*) This will take just a few minutes. If you'd like to wait in my office ...

ANDREW. Do you have a TV?

LAMB. No.

DOUGLAS. We'll hang out here.

(*During this conversation JIMMY has gone over to the casket. HE puts his arms under Mr. Campbell and starts lifting him out of the casket.*)

LAMB. (*Observing with horror.*) No!

(*HE regrets this outburst, as EVERYONE turns to see what is occurring. LAMB moves swiftly up to Jimmy, and speaks in a low voice.*)

LAMB. We'll be moving the whole casket.
JIMMY. Oh. (*JIMMY puts Mr. Campbell back in the casket. HE tries to set the body in its original position.*)
LAMB. (*Sharply.*) Leave him alone!

(*LAMB shuts the casket lid. JIMMY clears away the
     kneeler. THEY wheel the casket out.
SHARON intercepts them.*)

SHARON. (*Removing the floral blanket from the casket.*) These are *our* flowers.

(*LAMB pushes the casket while JIMMY carefully steers it
     through the doors. THEY exit.
There is a general pause.*)

ANDREW. Makes the room seem kind of empty, doesn't it?
SHARON. (*To Douglas.*) Well, are you satisfied? You couldn't go to Whiteside's funeral parlor, where Ma was waked, and Grandma and Grandpa; where they know what a Porteus looks like. No, you had to find the most expensive mortuary in the county.
DOUGLAS. These prices are competitive. They bleed you wherever you go. Besides, I have it on good authority that Whiteside's has a problem with rats. I don't trust funeral parlors with rats. I'd like to know what they're eating. At least this place has a little class.
SHARON. When they're not playing musical bodies.
DOUGLAS. So the guy's having a bad day. I'll get him to knock something off the bill, and we'll all come out ahead.

GLORIA. Personally, I can't understand how you can even talk about money at a time like this.

SHARON. Because it's not your money.

GLORIA. Maybe my family is different ...

DOUGLAS. (*A sarcastic laugh.*) *Maybe.*

GLORIA. (*Continuing.*) But in times of crisis we pull together. That's what family is all about. We put our petty differences aside, and we give each other support, and we observe the prescribed rituals, and, with the grace of God, everyone has a very nice time. I don't think we ever had a bad funeral.

DOUGLAS. What about your Uncle Tony's wake, when your aunt tried to climb into the coffin with him? (*To Andrew.*) She wanted to find out how stiff he really was.

(*THEY laugh.*)

GLORIA. That's not funny. The poor thing was overcome.

DOUGLAS. She was loaded.

GLORIA. You don't appreciate real emotion. When someone passes away he leaves a very big hole, and it's up to everyone else to fill that hole. Family, and community. The neighbors bring cakes, pastries, creampuffs, cannolis ... at least that's how we do it in Queens.

DOUGLAS. Queens is a wonderful place to be dead.

SHARON. *We're* going to have cold cuts tomorrow, after the cemetery.

GLORIA. My mother always tries to have *hot* food. It shows that you're making an effort. Your father only dies once, you know. And you're going to miss him.

(*SHARON, sobered by this thought, takes out her handkerchief and starts crying. GLORIA is satisfied.*)

GLORIA. That's better.

(*LAMB and JIMMY re-enter, wheeling in the new casket.*)

LAMB. The good news is, he's wearing his blue suit. And he has the most beatific smile you've ever seen!
   DOUGLAS. (*To the others.*) He does look good.

(*LAMB and JIMMY set the casket in place. LAMB opens
   the lid of the casket to reveal the true Mr. Porteus.
As the FAMILY approaches to view the body, LAMB holds
   them off.*)

LAMB. Give me a second.

(*THEY step back and wait as LAMB fusses with the body.
As LAMB looks into the casket, HE turns rather pale.
   Trying to be as inconspicuous as possible, HE reaches
   into the casket and pulls out a small toy fire-truck. HE
   hurriedly passes it to JIMMY, who hides it behind his
   back. LAMB steps away now and presents Mr. Porteus
   with a sweeping arm gesture.
The FAMILY gathers about the casket, murmuring with
   approval and recognition.
Moving away from the group, LAMB lets his smile fade.
   HE drops wearily into a chair, as JIMMY draws up
   beside him.*)

LAMB. What a catastrophe. Twenty-five years in this

business, and I've never seen such a thorough violation of that delicate spell of dreamlike contemplation, which is the mortician's trust.

JIMMY. They seem to be taking it in good spirits.

LAMB. Their nerves are deadened by grief. In the cold light of morning they'll reconsider their magnanimity. They can turn on you like *that*. (*HE snaps his fingers to demonstrate.*) I'll have to find someone to blame.

JIMMY. You can blame me if you want.

LAMB. There's no point in blaming a relative—that doesn't deflect the bullet very far. We can always pin it on the cleaning lady; she doesn't speak English anyway.

JIMMY. (*Remembering.*) I forgot about that guy on the phone. We don't bury animals, right?

LAMB. Of course not.

JIMMY. Under any circumstances?

LAMB. Well ... find out what kind of money he's talking about, and I'll get back to him.

JIMMY. (*Turns to go, and then stops.*) Oh, and what about Yolanda?

LAMB. Yolanda?

JIMMY. The girl I was telling you about.

LAMB. Oh, with the silken tendrils ...

JIMMY. I have to let her know about tonight.

LAMB. I simply can't spare you. You'd better accept the fact that you're an indispensable part of this operation. (*Seeing JIMMY's disappointment.*) This girl means a lot to you, does she?

JIMMY. Well ... as far as tonight is concerned, yes.

LAMB. There's an old saying in this business, son: Women will keep.

(As SHARON kneels to say a prayer, the OTHERS drift away from the casket. LAMB lowers his voice.)

LAMB. You'd better take care of that phone call. And find out what kind of an animal. If it's a cat, forget it. I hate cats.

(JIMMY exits into the office. LAMB turns to the family.)

LAMB. I'm sure you'd like to be alone at this very emotional time. If you'll excuse me, I'll re-set Mr. Campbell on his pillow. *(LAMB exits into the hallway.)*

ANDREW. Weird character, huh?

DOUGLAS. *(To Gloria.)* And when are your dear parents coming? Tonight?

GLORIA. I'm not sure they're coming at all.

DOUGLAS. What do you mean, they're not coming? Not that I'm dying to see them, but I would think out of common courtesy ...

GLORIA. Mama doesn't feel very well. She woke up this morning with one of those big pimples inside her nose ...

ANDREW. That can be extremely painful. There's nothing worse than a nasal obstruction.

DOUGLAS. And what's your father's excuse? Is he suffering from an overdose of garlic?

SHARON. *(Has risen from the casket kneeler.)* Will you please keep it down? You're making enough noise to ... *(SHE catches herself.)* Douglas ... *(SHE points towards the casket.)*

DOUGLAS. *(Unenthusiastic.)* Oh, my turn? *(HE approaches the casket and kneels.)*

SHARON. *(Dabbing at her eyes with the handkerchief.)*

What a terrible day. I'll be glad when it's over.

GLORIA. You and your father were very close, weren't you?

SHARON. I like to think we were. He always used to call me "Princess." Because he said I looked like Grace Kelly. (*Suddenly weeping.*) No one else will ever say that to me ... ! (*SHE turns away in tears.*)

(*DOUGLAS rises from the casket.*)

GLORIA. That's it?

DOUGLAS. I knew what I wanted to say. (*Regarding Sharon's crying.*) How did you get her started again?

GLORIA. She's upset because no one will ever say that she looks like Grace Kelly.

DOUGLAS. That's a revelation-and-a-half. (*Notices that ANDREW is moving towards the hall door.*) Hey, where are you going?

ANDREW. Get some fresh air. This place is like a sealed tomb.

DOUGLAS. I've heard that line before. You'll come back so full of fresh air that you'll be floating.

ANDREW. (*Resenting this.*) You think I'm sneaking out to get high or something?

DOUGLAS. Only took you one guess, didn't it?

ANDREW. Thanks an awful lot. It's good to know that my family has such complete trust in me. You want to search me? (*To Gloria.*) You want to search me?

(*GLORIA reaches out to frisk him. DOUGLAS intercedes.*)

DOUGLAS. Gloria, go say a prayer, will you? (*HE

pushes Gloria towards the casket, and returns to Andrew.) Don't think you can fool me with that choir boy act. You used to pull the same thing when you were stealing change off my bedroom dresser.

SHARON. (*Interrupting*.) Please, let's try to avoid memory lane. I've already talked to Andrew, and he assures me that he'll be on his best behavior. Why don't we give him the benefit of the doubt?

DOUGLAS. Because he's a liar.

ANDREW. You know, you used to irritate me when you said things like that, but now I just say to myself, "Hey, he's an asshole."

DOUGLAS. I'm making more money than you'll ever see.

ANDREW. And we're all so proud of you. You've made the Porteus name a household word. Actually you hear it more in the back seat of a car ...

DOUGLAS. Listen, there's nothing shameful about selling condoms. It's a legitimate and praiseworthy concern. If more people wore condoms, the world wouldn't be in such a sorry state.

SHARON. Now that's *enough*. We're not hear to talk about such disgusting things.

DOUGLAS. They're not disgusting. They're sanitary. And they're going to make me rich. The condom market is about to explode, mark my words.

ANDREW. Speaking of money, what's going on with the will? Who gets what?

SHARON. We don't know yet, Andy. It's only been two days.

ANDREW. I know, but he made out the will a long time ago. It's all on paper, right?

DOUGLAS. I suppose he made me the executor. Another headache ...

SHARON. No, I'm the executor.

DOUGLAS. (*Surprised.*) You are?

SHARON. The executrix, actually.

DOUGLAS. I didn't know that.

SHARON. So the lawyer tells me.

DOUGLAS. You've been talking to Klenkel already?

SHARON. Yes, we had to settle a few matters about the funeral, and the cemetery and such.

DOUGLAS. He called you?

SHARON. I guess so. We used the phone.

DOUGLAS. But *he* called *you*? You didn't call him?

SHARON. I don't remember who called who. What does that have to do with it? But he said that the will is clearly set forth in its intentions, and that there's no question as to its legality, and I'm the executrix. And we'll probably get together next week to find out where we stand.

ANDREW. So who gets the clock in the dining room? That's worth a lot of money.

SHARON. I don't know, Andrew.

ANDREW. You'll probably get all the furniture. What kind of a car did he have? Not that old Dodge Dart, still?

SHARON. He was too sick to drive a car. He got rid of the Dodge over two years ago.

ANDREW. No car, huh?

DOUGLAS. Did Klenkel say anything about the empty lot on Elm Avenue ... ?

SHARON. He didn't say anything. He said I'm the executrix.

DOUGLAS. Yeah, we heard that.

SHARON. I'm sure that whatever Daddy decided to do

with his property, he was fair and impartial. He was a good man ... (*Tears well up in SHARON's eyes, and SHE has to turn away.*)

DOUGLAS. (*Taking ANDREW aside.*) Something funny is going on here. I talked to Klenkel myself yesterday, and he didn't say anything about executors or executrixes.

ANDREW. He called you?

DOUGLAS. Never mind that. Why would she have to discuss the funeral with him? I was the one who was making all the arrangements. You remember him, don't you? Larry Klenkel?

ANDREW. His sister was in my class. Judy Klenkel. She was wild.

DOUGLAS. He's recently divorced, you know. His second wife.

ANDREW. Judy wore black underwear. I think she was in one of those Satanic cults.

DOUGLAS. Are you listening to me? He's divorced. And Sharon's divorced. And now they're calling each other up on the phone, and having secret meetings, and getting very cozy, it seems to me.

ANDREW. How do you know they're having secret meetings?

DOUGLAS. I *don't* know. Because they're *secret*.

ANDREW. So you're afraid she's getting romantically involved?

DOUGLAS. I don't care if she's screwing him six ways from Sunday. I only care about that will. And if they put their heads together—or anything else together—they can ace you and me right out the back door.

ANDREW. What about Judy? Is she still available?

DOUGLAS. (*Annoyed.*) Did you pay attention to

anything I just said?

ANDREW. Hey, look, I'm single, I have my own priorities.

(*GLORIA rises from the casket and rejoins the group.*)

DOUGLAS. (*To Gloria.*) I thought you fell asleep over there.

GLORIA. They really did an excellent job. He looks ten years younger.

DOUGLAS. He's still dead. (*Indicates Sharon, who is still crying.*) See what you can do with her, will you? (*GLORIA sits down with Sharon.*) It's all an act, if you ask me ...

(*DOUGLAS turns to Andrew as HE speaks, and finds that ANDREW is no longer there. ANDREW is just opening the doors, ready to sneak out.*)

DOUGLAS. Hey!

ANDREW. (*Standing in the doorway.*) There's a nice draft here.

DOUGLAS. It's about time you had your private moment with Dad. (*HE directs Andrew towards the casket.*)

ANDREW. (*Not exactly thrilled.*) Absolutely. I'm psyched.

(*ANDREW walks over to the casket and kneels. DOUGLAS checks on SHARON and GLORIA, who are whispering quietly. DOUGLAS takes a flask of whiskey from his pocket, and exits into the lobby.*)

SHARON. (*To Gloria.*) I wasn't even with him. He died alone, in bed. And I was ... I was somewhere else. It must have been horrible.

GLORIA. But he died in his sleep. That's a blessing.

SHARON. Suppose he wasn't sleeping? Suppose he woke up in pain, and he lay there in the darkness, crying for help. "Princess, Princess ... !" This is going to haunt me the rest of my life. (*Looking carefully at Gloria.*) Is that a new dress?

GLORIA. Yes, I bought it last month for my high-school reunion. I figured I could wear it again because I don't expect to see the same people here.

SHARON. It's very flattering to your figure.

GLORIA. I'm one of those people who happen to look good in anything. (*Indicates Sharon's dress.*) I've seen this before.

SHARON. I haven't had a new dress in years. Jerry never bought me anything.

GLORIA. How is Jerry? Do you ever see him?

SHARON. No, I don't see him. I don't want to be within a hundred miles of that man. I hate his guts.

GLORIA. I always thought that Jerry Muldoon was so good-looking. I wonder what he's doing now?

SHARON. Hopefully he's lying in some alleyway, living in a cardboard box, providing warmth and shelter to homeless cockroaches. Oh, if God would only do that for me ... !

DOUGLAS. (*Returns from the hallway, tucking the flask back into his pocket.*) It's almost three o'clock. Time to greet the public.

GLORIA. (*Rising.*) Do you think there'll be a crowd?

DOUGLAS. Not this afternoon. Probably just all the old retired farts. With the exception of your parents.

SHARON. Oh, they're not coming?

DOUGLAS. There's been an outbreak of nose pimples in Bayside. People are dropping like flies.

GLORIA. They're going to try to make the Mass tomorrow.

DOUGLAS. (*Looking around.*) I notice we didn't get many flowers.

SHARON. We didn't want flowers, remember? In the obituary we asked everyone to send a check to the American Cancer Society.

DOUGLAS. Which was stupid, since he died of a heart attack.

SHARON. But he had cancer.

DOUGLAS. He didn't die of it! They should have sent flowers anyway, because you know damn well that they're not sending any checks.

SHARON. (*Pointing, in a whisper.*) Look.

(*THEY all look at ANDREW, who is hunched over the casket, deep in prayer.*)

SHARON. I think that down deep he loved Daddy very much.

(*Unobserved, ANDREW suddenly lifts his head and takes a deep snort. HE shakes his head, and then glances around furtively, while gingerly brushing his nose. HE resumes a prayerful attitude.*)

LAMB. (*Enters from the hallway.*) We'll be opening

shortly. I know Father Gordon from St. Dominic's will be holding a short service this evening, but if you like I can say a few words now, to sort of set the tone for the afternoon's proceedings.

DOUGLAS. Free?

LAMB. It's included in the package.

SHARON. That would be nice. But let's wait until a few people show up.

DOUGLAS. Right. Why waste it on just the four of us?

LAMB. As you wish. If you would care to arrange yourselves on the far side of the casket, allowing a clear path to the Beloved ...

DOUGLAS. (*Taps Andrew on the shoulder.*) Are you finished?

ANDREW. (*As if snapping out of a trance, HE speaks with sudden energy.*) What? Yes! Yes! (*ANDREW bounds to his feet.*)

SHARON. We're receiving visitors now.

ANDREW. Good! Super!

(*THEY start to form a reception line.*)

SHARON. Should we do this by height?

DOUGLAS. You stand at the front. You're the daughter.

GLORIA. The oldest son should be at the head of the line. That's how we do it in my family.

SHARON. Andrew, put your jacket on.

ANDREW. (*With a glassy-eyed grin.*) My pleasure.

(*JIMMY returns from the office.*)

LAMB. Oh, there you are.

JIMMY. I was talking to Yolanda. She's all pissed off at me because I can't pick her up until ten-thirty. We had a big fight, and now she doesn't want to ever see me again.

LAMB. Did you explain to her that you would be busy tonight, cauterizing the wounds of grief and shepherding souls to a place of eternal peace and bliss without measure?

JIMMY. Not in so many words, no.

LAMB. Well, that's how you have to talk to these women. Appeal to their mystical instincts. Common sense won't do you a shred of good. Your mother, for example, had only a passing acquaintance with the rational world.

JIMMY. Come on, Dad, don't bring that up. I know you're bitter, but I'm sure Mom had her reasons for doing what she did, and I think we should try to be more understanding.

LAMB. She's a wonderful woman. I only hope that one day I get the chance to embalm her ... That reminds me: what about the dead animal?

JIMMY. It's a Rottweiler.

LAMB. That's a cat, isn't it?

JIMMY. No, it's a big dog.

LAMB. What did he offer?

JIMMY. He said that money is no object.

LAMB. What a noble sentiment. It takes my breath away.

JIMMY. I told him to bring the beloved remains over tomorrow morning.

LAMB. Good boy. But now what about this air-conditioning? Where is that goddamned electrician?

(As LAMB speaks, a large, muscular man in an orange

work suit enters from the hallway. HE is BOBBY GELARDI, the air-conditioning-and-refrigeration specialist. HE is a menacing figure, despite the friendly "BOBBY" which is scripted across the left pocket of his uniform.)

GELARDI. (*In a deep, ominous voice.*) I'm not an electrician. I'm an air-conditioning-and-refrigeration specialist.

LAMB. (*Just a bit intimidated.*) Have a nice lunch?

GELARDI. Chinese.

LAMB. A wise choice. Something light on a ferociously warm afternoon. We were just remarking that it's getting a bit humid in here ...

GELARDI. I said I'd fix it and I'll fix it. Don't push me.

LAMB. No, no, don't rush ... (*Reading his name.*) Bobby. I appreciate your attention to detail. But my customers are getting a tad uncomfortable ...

GELARDI. (*Horrified.*) Is that a dead body?

LAMB. That's Mr. Porteus. He's in repose ...

(GELARDI swoons into a faint.)

LAMB & JIMMY. A fainter!

(LAMB quickly breaks out a vial of smelling salts and waves it under Gelardi's nose.)

GELARDI. (*Coming to.*) Keep them away ... I don't want to die ... Save me, save me ... (*Staring at his hands.*) Blood! Blood! Blood!

(*As JIMMY restrains him, LAMB glances over at the Porteus family.*)

LAMB. (*Mustering a smile.*) He's going to fix the air-conditioner. (*To Jimmy.*) Quick, get him in the office. Fainters can be contagious, and then we'll have a real problem.

(*JIMMY hustles GELARDI into the office.*)

GELARDI. (*As HE leaves.*) The stench, the smell of rotting flesh ... !

(*JIMMY and GELARDI exit.*)

LAMB. (*Wiping his brow with a handkerchief.*) I have a bad feeling about this wake. (*HE consults his watch, and turns to the Porteus family.*) It's three o'clock.

(*THEY line up beside the casket: SHARON first, followed by DOUGLAS, GLORIA, and ANDREW. ALL assume positions of solemnity.*)

SHARON. We're ready.

(*LAMB draws a deep breath, walks over to the main doors, and solemnly swings them open. HE stands by the door, hands folded, waiting expectantly. After a lengthy pause, the LIGHTS dim.*)

Scene 2

That evening, about a quarter to nine.
SHARON is still standing dutifully by the casket. SHE
  looks exhausted.
DOUGLAS is flipping through the register book.
GLORIA sits on a folding chair, fanning herself with a
  Mass card.
ANDREW is in an armchair, sleeping.
There is no one else in the room. A small electric fan is by
  the window, which is cracked open.

DOUGLAS. (*Looking at the register.*) Seventeen names. And three "Mr. and Mrs.", so that makes an even twenty. The man lived seventy-two years, and twenty people come to his wake.

SHARON. Plus the four of us.

GLORIA. My parents would have made twenty-two.

DOUGLAS. A disgrace! An insult to his memory! Where was Joe Fabiano? Where was Artie Nagel—his best friend?

SHARON. Artie's in a nursing home now. In a wheelchair.

DOUGLAS. There's a ramp outside. And what happened to all the Murrays? Usually you can't turn around at a family function without falling over a Murray.

GLORIA. We had three tables of Murrays at our wedding.

DOUGLAS. And a lush, every one of them. If we had a portable bar in here we'd be beating them back with sticks.

GLORIA. I was surprised to see your Uncle Jack. I think he'll be next. He looks awful.

SHARON. He's looked awful for the last thirty years.

ANDREW. (*Roused from his slumber.*) And not one decent quail in the whole bunch. The only girl under forty was built like a fire hydrant.

SHARON. She was a nun.

ANDREW. She was? Oh ... Well, no loss, then.

(JIMMY enters from the hallway.)

DOUGLAS. (*To Jimmy.*) How's it going in the other rooms?

JIMMY. The Campbell wake is a madhouse. Wall-to-wall people. And with the heat, it's like a cattle car. And there's a steady turnover for Mrs. Hartigan. (*Pause.*) You know, you don't have to stay until nine. If you don't think anyone else is coming ...

SHARON. It's only fifteen more minutes. We might as well stick it out. Unless you have something you'd rather be doing ...

JIMMY. No, no—It's just that the sooner I can clean up ... You see, I'm supposed to meet someone in Commack ... Not that I'm trying to rush you out. It's your father, you take as much time as you want.

DOUGLAS. Gee, thanks.

GLORIA. (*Taking an interest.*) A girlfriend?

JIMMY. Sort of. She has beautiful skin.

GLORIA. How does she deal with the fact that you spend most of your time in the company of dead people? Does it bother her?

JIMMY. Well, she doesn't know. I haven't told her.

ANDREW. Never tell them anything.

DOUGLAS. Nonsense. Are you ashamed to be working in a mortuary?

JIMMY. It's not what I envisioned for myself.

DOUGLAS. Hey—it's a living. I'm in condoms myself. Some people think there's some kind of stigma attached to the condom business, but I'm up-front about it. I'm making an honest buck, and I'm filling a public need. What more could a man hope for? Now this girl of yours, she's on intimate terms with you? She satisfies your basic urges?

JIMMY. (*Embarrassed.*) Well ...

DOUGLAS. We're both men of the world. Do you use condoms?

JIMMY. Uh ... actually ...

DOUGLAS. I see. It's not your responsibility. You can't get pregnant. Did you ever hear of AIDS? Did you ever hear of plague? Did you ever hear of the Black Death? I'm not trying to scare you, but you could be living on borrowed time. I know what you're going to say: they're not comfortable, they don't feel natural ... but have you ever tried a Porteus Portable?

JIMMY. No.

DOUGLAS. (*Hands him a business card.*) All right, then. Porteus Portables. Condoms with a conscience. Genuine lamb skin latex, fits like a velvet glove. We're bringing out a whole line of designer colors: yellow, lime-green, day-glo red. And they're biodegradable.

ANDREW. Let's keep the schoolyards clean.

DOUGLAS. I have some fresh samples in the car. (*DOUGLAS exits into the hallway.*)

JIMMY. This really isn't necessary.

ANDREW. Don't look a gift horse in the mouth. (*Takes*

JIMMY aside.) Listen, you need anything?

JIMMY. What do you mean?

ANDREW. You know ... *Anything.* Coke. Grass. Percodan. Super-crack ...

JIMMY. I don't do drugs.

ANDREW. Good! Drugs are a poisonous habit. Public Enemy Number One. So many of my friends have fallen victim to the ravages of substance abuse ... it breaks my heart ...

(ANDREW shakes his head and exits into the hallway, as LAMB enters.)

LAMB. (*To Jimmy, as HE wipes the perspiration from his face.*) Do me a favor. Get about six air-fresheners from the office and put them in the Rose Room. I think Mr. Campbell is starting to react.

JIMMY. Is the crowd breaking up yet?

LAMB. Just about. The firemen just officially retired his helmet and shield. Now the Elks are giving the sacred toast. "Wherever an Elk may roam ... ", so on and so forth. I never shook so many sweaty palms in my life—my shirt-cuff is soaked. Have you checked with the electrician, or whatever he calls himself?

JIMMY. He says don't rush him. This is going to cost a fortune in overtime, you know.

LAMB. We have to get it fixed. It's supposed to hit 98 tomorrow. (*HE sniffs the air.*) You'd better get an air-freshener for here, too. Seems a bit stale.

(JIMMY exits into the office. LAMB turns to the two women.)

LAMB. Well, it's been a long night. I'm sorry I couldn't spend more time with you, but I had my hands full inside. I thought Father Gordon handled the service very well.

SHARON. Do we have to pay him for that?

LAMB. I'm sure he won't discourage your contributions. That was a funny story he told, about your father putting the lottery ticket in the collection basket, and the number coming in. That must have killed him ... so to speak.

SHARON. That never happened. Father Gordon tells that story all the time. He just changes the names.

LAMB. Well, it's still a funny story. For a priest, anyway.

(JIMMY comes out of the office, carrying air-fresheners, as the PHONE rings offstage.)

JIMMY. Dad, the phone ...

(JIMMY puts an air-freshener on the lamp table and exits into the hallway. LAMB exits into the office to answer the phone.)

GLORIA. (*Admiringly.*) He has such a droll sense of humor.

SHARON. Yeah, he's a riot.

GLORIA. Would you ever consider having an affair with a mortician?

SHARON. No, I don't think I would.

GLORIA. Just for curiosity's sake. They must know things that we don't.

SHARON. There are some subjects upon which I prefer to remain ignorant. I'm sure that Mr. Lamb is a normal man with reasonable appetites, but his hands are so *cold*, even in this weather ...

GLORIA. Well ... Cold hands, warm heart.

SHARON. (*A sly smile.*) It wasn't his *heart* I was thinking about.

(GLORIA and SHARON giggle at this suggestive remark. ANDREW returns from the hallway, a dazed, stoned expression on his face. Seeing the women laughing, HE joins in, without knowing why. SHARON sees him and stops laughing.)

SHARON. Where did you go?

ANDREW. (*Loudly.*) I went for a walk!

SHARON. (*Recognizing the symptoms.*) Why don't you wait for us in the car?

ANDREW. Why? I'm fine!

(LAMB enters from the office, in noticeably good humor. SHARON takes Andrew aside and talks to him quietly. LAMB glances at Gloria, and THEY exchange smiles.)

GLORIA. Was there good news on the phone?

LAMB. Yes, for a change. A six-year-old girl was hit by a car.

GLORIA. That's *terrible* news.

LAMB. Hmm? Oh. Yes, terrible. *Tragic.* But it does come at a good time. There are certain hard economic realities in the funeral industry today. Competition is fierce, and the scramble for fresh bodies can be ruthless in the extreme. I have a few connections—an intern at the hospital, a police sergeant—and they keep me abreast of the latest developments.

GLORIA. My husband was telling me that one funeral parlor is infested with rats.

LAMB. You mean Whitesides? That's only a vicious rumor. Don't expect me to confirm it. I can only say that here at the Good Shepherd we have never had a problem with vermin.

GLORIA. What about your wife? Does she help out, too?

LAMB. My wife is no longer with us.

GLORIA. She passed away?

LAMB. No, she ran off with a casket salesman. I don't want to discuss it. (*JIMMY enters from the hallway.*) Oh, Jimmy ... After we clean up, you have to make a pick-up at the Community Hospital.

JIMMY. What?

LAMB. A little girl has seen the face of God. If we can start preparation tonight we might be able to slip her in tomorrow afternoon. (*To Gloria.*) These one-day wakes are killing us. In the old days we'd have a body in repose for at least three days. We have to make it up in volume.

JIMMY. But I can't go. I have to pick up Yolanda in Commack.

LAMB. Again with this Yolanda? I thought she never wanted to see you again.

JIMMY. She still wants me to pick her up.

LAMB. We've got a *business* to run here ...

(*JIMMY storms into the office in disgust.*
LAMB sighs with resignation, and turns back to Gloria.)

LAMB. Some young hairless thing has captured his fancy. He's at that point in his life where his judgment is clouded by glandular secretions. When he's spent as many hours in the embalming room as I have, he'll come to acquire a more unsentimental view of the corporeal mysteries. The choicest flesh is subject to decay, whereas the soul, by dint of its very insubstantiality, eludes the bacterial mandate and soars giddily into eternity. (*HE stares at Gloria's breasts.*) You see, I'm a firm believer in the duality of nature ... (*LAMB wipes his brow.*) Excuse me ... I need a dry handkerchief ... (*LAMB rises quickly and exits into the hall.*)

ANDREW. (*Raising his voice as he talks to Sharon.*) There's nothing wrong with me! My behavior has been impeccable!

SHARON. Your eyes don't look focused.

ANDREW. I'll focus my eyes as soon as there's something worth focusing on.

DOUGLAS. (*Enters from the hallway.*) Where's the kid? I've got some top-of-the-line product here. (*To Andrew.*) Need a box?

ANDREW. (*Taking a box of condoms.*) Can never have enough.

DOUGLAS. (*Offering a box.*) Sharon?

SHARON. What would I want with those?

DOUGLAS. They're tailored for the women's market. They have little bumps on them.

GLORIA. I recommend them highly.

DOUGLAS. (*To Gloria.*) Listen, it's almost nine. You want to get out of here?

GLORIA. We can't leave until visiting hours are over.

Do you want to hurt Mr. Lamb's feelings?

DOUGLAS. What's the point in hanging around? Nobody else is coming.

(An attractive blonde WOMAN in her mid-thirties, dressed in black, appears in the doorway.
EVERYONE falls silent at this unexpected vision.
THEY stare at her in bewilderment. SHE approaches the coffin and kneels.)

DOUGLAS. (*Whispering.*) Who's that?
ANDREW. She looks mighty good, whoever she is. (*HE puts the condoms in his jacket pocket.*) I'd better put these where I'll remember them.

(SHARON makes a scouting mission, stealing up furtively behind the Woman to get a close look at her. SHE tiptoes back to the others.)

SHARON. You know who that is? Norma Czerniawski!
DOUGLAS. What? It can't be!
SHARON. I should know—I went to school with her. (*With great conviction.*) I can't *stand* that woman.
DOUGLAS. I went to more than school with her, and she's a natural brunette.
ANDREW. That's right. You and Norma ...
GLORIA. What's this? Norma? You never told me about any Norma ...
DOUGLAS. (*Trying to downplay it.*) It was *high school.*
GLORIA. You told me all about high school. You told me about Barbara Schaefer, and Kelly what's-her-name, and that Walling girl who was double-jointed, and Judy

Klenkel ...

ANDREW. You laid Judy Klenkel? With the black underwear?

DOUGLAS. It was more like charcoal ...

GLORIA. But you never said anything about any Norma Chebusky.

SHARON. Czerniawski.

DOUGLAS. She had a crush on me. It was a schoolgirl infatuation. (*To the others.*) Right? (*There is no response.*)

SHARON. I suppose we ought to form a reception line for her.

(THEY form a line around the casket.)

DOUGLAS. (*Speaking low.*) We'll all shake her hand, and then we'll get rid of her.

GLORIA. What's the hurry? Afraid she'll say something incriminating?

ANDREW. She has great posture.

SHARON. She always did. She was Miss Perfect, the teacher's pet. She helped grade papers. Had perfect penmanship. Never chewed her fingernails. Never needed braces. Never picked her nose. Never had to go the bathroom. Everyone hated her.

(NORMA rises from the casket and turns to face SHARON, who produces a heartwarming smile.)

SHARON. Norma! How wonderful to see you!

NORMA. Hello, Sharon. (*Taking her hand.*) I'm so sorry.

SHARON. (*With a sigh.*) He's better off. The last few

years were very hard for him.

NORMA. He was a good man.

SHARON. We appreciate your stopping by.

NORMA. *(Moves on to Douglas. Taking his hand.)* Douggie ... I'm so sorry.

DOUGLAS. *(A shrug.)* What can you do?

(As DOUGLAS and NORMA smile at each other, GLORIA clears her throat.)

DOUGLAS. This is my wife, Gloria.

NORMA. *(Quickly shaking Gloria's hand.)* I'm so sorry. *(SHE moves on to Andrew.)* And little Andy ... I'm so sorry.

ANDREW. About what?

NORMA. About your father.

ANDREW. Oh. Yeah.

(NORMA turns and looks at the casket thoughtfully. SHE then walks slowly over to an armchair and sits down. SHE stares at the casket, while the OTHERS stand uncomfortably in place.)

SHARON. *(Her teeth clenched.)* Is she staying?

DOUGLAS. It looks that way.

GLORIA. Maybe someone should talk to her, "Douggie."

SHARON. No, she's a typical Polack; if she starts talking she'll never leave. Let's give her a few minutes.

ANDREW. I'm going to sit down.

(ANDREW pulls a chair over to his spot in line and sits.

THEY wait in silence.
After a moment, a GIRL of about twenty, with radiant skin,
  appears in the doorway. SHE looks searchingly about
  the room.)

DOUGLAS. (*Seeing the Girl.*) Jesus Christ, another one!
We'll never get out of here.

(The GIRL starts across the room towards them. As SHE
  passes the casket, SHE pauses self-consciously, and
  then kneels. SHE says a quick prayer, rises, and turns
  to Sharon.)

GIRL. Hi. I'm looking for Jimmy Lamb.
SHARON. He's in the Rose Room.
GLORIA. No, that's *Campbell*.
DOUGLAS. There's no Lamb on display tonight. Maybe
he's still on ice.

(JIMMY enters from the office. HE freezes as he spots the
  GIRL, who rushes to him.)

GIRL. Jimmy!
JIMMY. Yolanda! What are you doing here?
YOLANDA. I wanted to surprise you.
JIMMY. And a wonderful surprise it is. I was just trying
to call you ...
YOLANDA. I thought I'd save time by driving here. I
found your house—the big grey building with the black
trim, and the yew trees—No one was home, but a neighbor
said you'd be down here. What is it, a relative?
JIMMY. Yes, my uncle. Uncle ... (*HE reaches behind*

his back and takes a memorial card off the register stand.
He glances at the card surreptitiously.) ... Uncle Walter.
Old Uncle Walter.

YOLANDA. I'm so sorry.

JIMMY. He was a good man.

YOLANDA. But why didn't you tell me you had to go
to a wake?

JIMMY. I didn't want to depress you. You're such a
sensitive little mouse.

YOLANDA. And I said those terrible things to you ...

(YOLANDA throws her arms around Jimmy. DOUGLAS
    catches JIMMY's eye. HE offers to toss him a box of
    condoms. JIMMY shakes his head.)

JIMMY. *(Leading YOLANDA away.)* This is the funeral
director's office. We can be alone.

YOLANDA. You're so resourceful.

(JIMMY and YOLANDA exit.
The OTHERS remain standing at the casket, while
    NORMA sits motionless, her head now bowed in
    meditative silence.)

ANDREW. I don't think this strategy is working.

DOUGLAS. Somebody could pull the fire alarm.

SHARON. Maybe if we start saying our final prayers,
she'll get the hint.

DOUGLAS. *(Pained.)* More prayers?

ANDREW. *(Looks in the casket, raises his voice.)* See
you in the morning, Dad! Gotta go now! Big day
tomorrow! *(Pointedly to Norma.)* Time to go, everybody!

Last call!

SHARON. *(Embarrassed.)* Be quiet, will you?

ANDREW. I'm just trying to be helpful. *(Yelling.)* I'm leaving now! Who needs a ride?

LAMB. *(Enters hurriedly from the hallway.)* What's the problem in here?

SHARON. We were just getting ready to leave. (*SHE nods towards Norma.*)

LAMB. Oh, a lingerer? There's always one in the crowd who can't tear herself away from the grim spectacle. Who can explain or deny the morbid fascination that visits upon our dealings with the netherworld?

GLORIA. Beautifully put.

ANDREW. *(Pointing into the casket.)* Is this a real ring, or one of those cubic zirconia things you get in the mail?

LAMB. We don't approve of mock jewelry. The integrity of the Beloved is sacrosanct.

SHARON. That's Grandpa's old Celtic ring. See the funny cross there? It once belonged to Finn MacCool.

ANDREW. You mean that bar in Port Washington?

SHARON. No, Finn MacCool was a great Irish hero. He built Dublin, or something. And this ring was later blessed by St. Patrick himself. Grandpa found it in a pawnshop.

ANDREW. It must be worth some money, then. Don't you think we should take it home with us tonight, in case somebody breaks in?

DOUGLAS. Who's going to break into a funeral parlor?

ANDREW. I've done it.

LAMB. I can vouch for the ring's safety. And tomorrow we'll remove all the jewelry prior to the sealing of the casket.

SHARON. No, Daddy wanted to be buried with the ring.

ANDREW. He what?

SHARON. He wanted to be buried with Grandpa's Celtic ring. It's in the will.

DOUGLAS. How do you know it's in the will?

SHARON. I'm the executrix. It's my duty to see that the wishes of the deceased are properly disposed of.

DOUGLAS. Is that what it says in the will? What else does it say in the will? Does it say who's going to clean up, and who's going to be left out in the cold?

SHARON. I haven't seen the will. I only know what Larry told me.

DOUGLAS. Larry? Larry?

ANDREW. I don't mean to interrupt, but I think there's a law against burying precious antique rings, I really do.

LAMB. I would be skeptical about the authenticity of such a ring. Finn MacCool, for one thing, was a mythical character, and a giant mythical character at that. The likelihood that you could purchase a giant, mythical ring at a local pawnshop is remote at best ...

SHARON. (*Outraged.*) What are you talking about? This is my grandfather's Celtic ring!

DOUGLAS. Who asked you, anyway? Mind your own goddamn business!

ANDREW. Yeah!

(*LAMB, taken aback, moves away from them. As the THREE continue to argue quietly, GLORIA goes over to soothe Lamb's feelings.*)

LAMB. How dare they speak to me like that in my own funeral parlor?

GLORIA. Don't pay any attention to them. They're just

working out their grief.

LAMB. I realize this hasn't been the smoothest of wakes for them, but I've had my trials today, too. Not the least of which is that worthless air-conditioning specialist, who doesn't appear to know an electric socket from a hole in the wall.

(GELARDI enters from the hallway with his toolbox.)

LAMB. I've never seen such an incompetent, unmotivated, slow-witted buffoon ... (*HE sees Gelardi. Without missing a beat, HE pats Gelardi's shoulder.*) ... And I'm certainly glad we fired that fellow and brought in Bobby here to take care of things. (*Brightly.*) Anything I can get you? A drink? A sandwich?
GELARDI. No. It's fixed.
LAMB. Already?
GELARDI. You shouldn't have any more problems.

(The LIGHTS go out. Everything is plunged into DARKNESS.)

LAMB. I think this qualifies as a problem.
ANDREW. Am I having a blackout?
SHARON. Somebody turned out the lights. Must be a cost-cutting measure.
LAMB. Please, everyone remain calm. We must have blown a fuse. Do you have a flashlight in your toolbox? (*There is no response.*) Bobby? Where did he go? (*Reaching in the dark.*) Is that you?
GLORIA. No, it's me.
LAMB. Oh. Sorry.

DOUGLAS. Are you going to get some lights in here? You *must* have candles ...

LAMB. There's a flashlight in my office. Now please don't move. You might trip over something, or break something expensive. Just stay where you are, and I'll be right back. (*LAMB is heard crashing to the floor.*) Don't be alarmed. I just tripped over something. I'm perfectly all right.

DOUGLAS. (*Sarcastic.*) What a relief.

(*LAMB gasps with pain as HE limps over to the office and enters. A moment of silence.*
Suddenly there is a commotion in the office—SOUNDS of stumbling and confusion. YOLANDA screams.
The beam of a FLASHLIGHT appears, as LAMB emerges from the office. The first object the light falls upon is a shapely female leg. The LIGHT tracks up the body, discovering clothes in disarray. Finlly the LIGHT rests on Yolanda's face.)

LAMB. Who are you?
YOLANDA. I'm Yolanda.
LAMB. I had to ask.
JIMMY. She's with me.

(*LAMB turns the light on JIMMY, whose shirt is half-unbuttoned.*)

LAMB. Jimmy, get some candles out of the closet, will you?

(*JIMMY exits. LAMB starts across the room, and falls*

again with a CRASH.)

LAMB. Don't worry. I just tripped again. (*HE trains the flashlight on the obstruction, which turns out to be GELARDI, curled up in a fetal position, his hands covering his head.*) Mr. Gelardi? Bobby?

GELARDI. (*In a choked, terrified voice.*) Leave me alone! Turn on the lights!

LAMB. You're an electrician and you're afraid of the dark?

GELARDI. Save me ... ! The cold hands of death are squeezing my throat! I can't breathe!

LAMB. Why don't you just stay there for now? (*To the others.*) I'm going to check the fuse box. Please, don't anyone move!

(LAMB turns and falls over a chair. HE rises and exits into the hallway.
There is a moment of silence.)

SHARON. It's kind of creepy, sitting here in the dark next to a dead body. Even though it is Dad.

ANDREW. Maybe we should sing something.

GLORIA. That's an idea. Keep our spirits up.

SHARON. What should we sing?

ANDREW. How about a little Springsteen?

SHARON. We could sing a round. Like "Row, row, row your boat ... "

GLORIA. Well, first, who's singing? Douglas, are you going to sing?

DOUGLAS. (*With measured scorn.*) No, I am *not* going to sing.

GLORIA. Yolanda, you're welcome to sing with us.
YOLANDA. Thanks, but I'm not really part of the wake.
I'm just visiting.
SHARON. We should sing something for Daddy.
GLORIA. Yes, that would be nice.
SHARON. Let's sing Daddy's favorite song.
GLORIA. Okay, but I'm not sure I know all the words.
SHARON. I'll start, and you can all join in. Andrew?
ANDREW. I'll fake it.
SHARON. Ready?

(SHARON starts to sing a novelty song from the 40s, up-tempo and utterly inappropriate. After afew bars, GLORIA and ANDRREW join in. The song proceeds tentatively at first, but soon THEY get into the spirit of it, and start singing boisterously.
The LIGHTS come up, revealing SHARON, ANDREW, and GLORIA singing, as well as YOLANDA. Also singing is NORMA; SHE is, in fact, standing on her chair, and really belting out the lyrics. GELARDI still cowers on the floor, and DOUGLAS watches in disbelief.
The OTHERS stop singing, and look at NORMA, who continues with great gusto. SHE suddenly stops short, realizing that SHE is creating a spectacle.)

ANDREW. Now that's entertainment.

(NORMA climbs down from her chair and sits.)

DOUGLAS. Let's get the hell out of here.
ANDREW. Yeah, this party is history. So what do you
guys want to do now? A little bowling, some miniature

golf, perhaps ... ?

(As ANDREW moves away from the casket, HE inadvertently reveals that MR. PORTEUS' HAND is dangling out of the casket. The Celtic ring is missing from the finger. There is a general gasp from ALL. ANDREW turns and sees the hand.)

ANDREW. Good God! The ring is gone! What a shock! *(DOUGLAS stares at Andrew accusingly.)* Don't even say it. I can tell just by looking at you that you think I took the ring off Dad's finger while the lights were out. Why? Because I've had my troubles in the past, and so naturally I make a most convenient scapegoat. But let me remind you that this is America, where every man has a right to a fair trial by a jury of his peers ...
DOUGLAS. Give me that ring!
ANDREW. *(Circles behind the casket for protection.)* No need to raise your voice. Try to remember where you are.

(DOUGLAS pursues him, and THEY continue circling around the casket.
LAMB enters from the hallway.)

LAMB. *(A weary sigh.)* Please don't play around the casket. *(LAMB kneels beside Gelardi.)* Bobby? The lights are on. I shut off the air-conditioning system, and everything's going to be all right.
JIMMY. *(Enters from the office carrying an armful of candles.)* These are all the candles I could find. And I brought another air-freshener.

LAMB. Help me get Mr. Gelardi to his feet.
JIMMY. He fainted again?
LAMB. He seems to be cracking under the pressure of constant air-conditioning repair.

(*JIMMY and LAMB lift GELARDI to his feet and set him in a chair.*)

LAMB. Do you want someone to take you home?
GELARDI. (*Hands locked over his ears.*) Stop those voices! Those maddening voices! What do they want from me? Blood! Blood!
JIMMY. (*Whispering to Lamb.*) He's not riding in my car.
LAMB. No, you'd better call an ambulance. (*As JIMMY moves to exit.*) And ask them to bring that little girl with them. Kill two birds with one stone.
GELARDI. (*Suddenly rises and grabs Jimmy's arm.*) Where are you going?
LAMB. We're going to get you some help.
GELARDI. The police?
LAMB. No, no, a doctor ...
GELARDI. (*His eyes wide with terror.*) A doctor? A *medical* doctor? From a *hospital*?
LAMB. Well ... Yes, that's where they all hang out ...
GELARDI. You're not taking me back there! You'll have to kill me first!

(*GELARDI reaches into his toolbox and pulls out a gun.*

EVERYONE freezes.)

LAMB. Uh oh.
GELARDI. Don't make any false moves! Nobody leaves
this room alive.

BLACKOUT

END OF ACT I

ACT II

Scene 1

The Lilac Room.
Two seconds after the end of Act I.
EVERYONE is holding the same position.

GELARDI. (*Brandishing the gun wildly.*) All right, I want everyone together, with their hands up. Move! *(To Yolanda.)* You, too, sister.

YOLANDA. (*As SHE moves.*) I want you to know, I'm not related to these people in any way.

(*THEY assemble near the casket.*)

GELARDI. Don't bunch up like that. Spread out so I can see you.

(*THEY stand with their hands raised. Several long moments pass.*)

GLORIA. (*Sniffs the air.*) Somebody didn't use their under-arm deodorant this morning.

DOUGLAS. (*Under his breath.*) This is ridiculous. How do we know that gun's even loaded?

ANDREW. (*To Gelardi.*) Is that gun loaded?

*(GELARDI fires the gun at a religious statue, shattering
   it.
ANDREW turns to Douglas.)*

ANDREW. See, all you have to do is ask.
GELARDI. Now everyone slowly sit down. That way I
can keep an eye on you (*As THEY tentatively lower their
hands.*) I didn't say put your hands down!

*(THEY quickly raise their hands again, and find chairs.
ANDREW, still standing, vacillates between one chair and
   another.)*

ANDREW. I just can't decide.
GLORIA. Here, sit in the middle.

*(ANDREW sits between Sharon and Gloria, with Lamb on
   Gloria's other side.)*

GLORIA. That's perfect. Boy-girl, boy-girl.
GELARDI. (*Looks them over.*) I don't like it. Stand up
again. (*THEY stand.*) No, sit down.
DOUGLAS. Oh, come on, make up your mind!
GELARDI. Don't pressure me! All right, the men stand
up and the women sit down. (*HE considers this
arrangement a moment, and then shakes his head in
despair.*) I don't know what to do. I'm so confused.
LAMB. (*Steps forward.*) If I might make a suggestion,
why don't you let everyone find a position that is most
comfortable for him or her? Certainly there's nothing
threatening about us—we're not carrying any weapons, are
we?

ANDREW. I have a razor blade.

(*ANDREW holds up the razor blade. GELARDI snatches it. HE regards the others with mistrust, but HE relents.*)

GELARDI. All right—at ease. But remember, I'm watching you, and I'd just as soon kill a man as tighten a screw. I once strangled a guy with my bare hands because I didn't like the way the hairs stuck out of his nose.

LAMB. (*To the others.*) A word to the wise.

(*THEY all lower their arms and try to relax.*)

GELARDI. (*To Lamb.*) Sorry about the damage. I might as well confess, this is my first hostage situation. I'm likely to make mistakes.

LAMB. I don't think anyone noticed. Tell me, why are you holding us hostage?

GELARDI. It wasn't my idea. Ask him. (*HE points to the casket.*)

LAMB. Ask Mr. Porteus? (*Trying to mask his alarm.*) Is Mr. Porteus telling you what to do?

GELARDI. Can't you hear him? (*HE listens intently by the casket.*)

LAMB. Excuse me a moment. (*LAMB sidles over to the others.*) I don't wish to alarm anyone, but Mr. Gelardi is having conversations with the dead.

JIMMY. I guess we can forget about getting the air-conditioner fixed.

SHARON. What does he want from us?

LAMB. He doesn't know himself. He's taking orders from your father.

ANDREW. That's typical Dad. Always telling everybody what to do.

DOUGLAS. He always told *you* what to do because you never knew what the hell you were doing. He never told *me* what to do.

ANDREW. Because he never paid any attention to you. Because you're an asshole.

DOUGLAS. (*Enraged.*) You're an asshole!

ANDREW. You're an asshole!

LAMB. Gentlemen, must I remind you that we have a lunatic in the room?

ANDREW. Well, he started it.

GLORIA. He's awfully good-looking for a lunatic, though, isn't he?

GELARDI. What are you whispering about over there?

LAMB. (*Returning to Gelardi.*) Nothing. Casual small talk ...

GELARDI. Not you. Him! (*Yelling at Mr. Porteus.*) Speak up if you have something to say! (*To Lamb.*) He's plotting against me. He wants to take me with him. He wants to bury me!

LAMB. (*Trying to calm him.*) No, I'm sure you're mistaken. Why, he's just ... praying. He's saying a prayer for you.

GELARDI. You must think I'm crazy to believe a story like that. I know how these dead souls are. They're all the same. Out for my blood. Always they're calling me ... "Come to us, Bobby! Kill yourself, Bobby Kill everyone!"

LAMB. That must be very distracting. I don't blame you for feeling a bit edgy.

GELARDI. (*Exploding at him.*) What do you know about it? How do you know how I feel? You don't know how I feel! You don't know anything about me!

LAMB. (*Gently.*) I know that you're seriously deranged. Surely that must count for something.

GELARDI. Leave me alone! Let me wrestle with my demons!

LAMB. (*Withdrawing.*) Yes, you do that. Please let us know if you start losing. (*LAMB joins the others.*)

SHARON. What did he say?

LAMB. He's going to wrestle with his demons for a while.

DOUGLAS. Why do we have to stay and watch? I have business to take care of. Condoms are a twenty-four-hour concern.

SHARON. I still have to clean the house for the party after the cemetery.

GLORIA. And I haven't called Mama all day. I wonder how that pimple is?

DOUGLAS. Good God, I completely forgot about your mother's pimple! For all we know, it could have erupted into a boil by now!

LAMB. For the present, all we can do is wait.

(*JIMMY takes the opportunity to usher YOLANDA forward.*)

JIMMY. Dad, I don't think you've been formally introduced. This is my beloved, Yolanda Kamola.

YOLANDA. I'm sorry about your brother-in-law.

LAMB. (*Bewildered.*) My brother-in-law? My brother-in-law is dead.

YOLANDA. Yes, I know.

JIMMY. (*Changing the subject.*) How about her skin,

Dad? Didn't I tell you, smooth and milky?

YOLANDA. Do you have to tell everyone about my skin?

JIMMY. He's family.

YOLANDA. (*To Lamb*.) Jimmy seems to think I'm something special. In reality I'm just an ordinary well-adjusted young woman with exceptional skin texture. I can't take any credit for it—it's a gift from God.

LAMB. So nice to see religion making a comeback among our young people.

ANDREW. (*Sits down beside Norma*.) I hope you didn't have any plans for tonight. It looks like we might be stuck here for a while.

NORMA. I don't mind. The near presence of death fills me with a peaceful calm. I'm resigned to my fate.

ANDREW. (*Nods*.) That's deep. (*Lowers his voice*.) You need any drugs?

NORMA. I don't do drugs.

ANDREW. Good for you. (*HE walks away, muttering*.) Everyone's a fucking saint around here.

GLORIA. (*Observing Gelardi*.) Do you suppose he really is communicating with your father's spirit? I mean, he looks like he's talking to *someone*.

SHARON. I think if Daddy were to talk to anyone, he would talk to me.

DOUGLAS. (*To Lamb*.) Didn't he mention something about killing himself?

LAMB. Yes, the voices have suggested that.

DOUGLAS. Maybe we should encourage him in that direction. It would resolve matters to my satisfaction.

LAMB. But what an awful mess it would make. We just painted the walls ... !

DOUGLAS. He doesn't have to shoot himself. There are cleaner methods. Poison, for example. You must have a wide assortment of toxic chemicals at your disposal.

LAMB. I can't assume an active role in Mr. Gelardi's suicide. That would present a conflict of interest.

GLORIA. (*Agreeing.*) You can't expect him to violate his business ethics.

DOUGLAS. (*With disgust.*) As if at this point I really give a shit.

LAMB. (*Privately, to Gloria.*) How could I have let this situation get so out of hand?

GLORIA. It's not your fault. This could have happened at any funeral parlor.

LAMB. No, no, it's my responsibility. I'm supposed to be in control. I don't know what's the matter with me lately. I must be suffering Mortician's Burnout ...

SHARON. Mr. Lamb, do you think you could possibly put my father's hand back in the coffin where it belongs? It looks a bit effeminate, you know?

LAMB. (*To Gloria.*) You see what I mean? I didn't even notice that Mr. Porteus was hanging out of the casket. When you start to overlook the fine details, maybe it's time to get out.

(*LAMB tends to Mr. Porteus, while GLORIA watches. SHARON approaches Norma.*)

SHARON. Norma, I couldn't help but notice that you've been awfully quiet tonight. I hope you're not getting depressed on our account. I mean, we appreciate the sympathy, but you don't have to go overboard.

NORMA. I just can't believe that he's gone. He was so

youthful, so full of life.

SHARON. You remember him from high school. Things change. He was in his early seventies, and pretty well shot. Cancer, arthritis, bursitis, phlebitis ... the last few years I had my hands full with him. Not that I'm complaining, mind you; I know that I'll get my reward ... But, Good Lord, the sheer aggravation—I didn't have a life of my own.

NORMA. Is that why your husband ran off on you?

SHARON. (*Brought up short.*) I beg your pardon?

NORMA. Jerry Muldoon—I understand he left you.

SHARON. (*Keeping her composure.*) Jerry and I are divorced, it's true, but it was a mutual separation, and we're still on very good terms. You never married, did you?

NORMA. No.

SHARON. What a shame. You were such a pretty girl. Well, maybe the blonde hair will change your luck.

(*GLORIA watches with fascination as LAMB fusses with Mr. Porteus.*)

GLORIA. It's amazing the way you just thread that rosary between his fingers.

LAMB. It's not difficult. Takes a little practice.

GLORIA. And how do you get that healthy glow in the cheeks? I've been trying to achieve that for years.

LAMB. We have our little magic tricks. Actually a great deal depends on the effects of the embalming fluid. Sometimes it turns the skin green, and then you've got a job on your hands.

GLORIA. What would you suggest for me? I have such

problems with cosmetic balance.

LAMB. I'm not really qualified to deal with living organisms.

GLORIA. For instance, I have these oil spots on my forehead, and my nose ... (*SHE takes LAMB's hand and runs his fingers along her nose. LAMB nods in recognition.*) But then I have these dry patches on my cheeks, and my jaw ... And even down here ... (*SHE directs LAMB's hand to the exposed area directly above her breasts.*) Doesn't it feel awful?

LAMB. (*Nervously.*) Yes ... I may have some creams to relieve this problem ...

(*LAMB turns, and finds DOUGLAS behind him, watching with interest. LAMB smiles sheepishly.*)

LAMB. I was feeling her dry patches.

DOUGLAS. Yeah, she's got them all over. Look, are we going to wait all night for this guy to blow his brains out?

LAMB. What else can we do?

DOUGLAS. You have a phone in your office. Call the police.

LAMB. What a good idea. Maybe Mr. Gelardi will dial the number for me.

DOUGLAS. What, are you afraid? (*HE spots JIMMY, engaged in some heavy romancing with YOLANDA.*) Hey, Romeo. (*HE hands JIMMY the box of condoms.*) Here's the package I promised you. Untouched by human hands.

JIMMY. (*Flustered.*) You don't have to ...

DOUGLAS. Don't mention it. Your pleasure is my business. You want to do me a favor in return? There's a phone in your old man's office ...

GLORIA. You can't send him in there. He's only a kid.

DOUGLAS. If he's old enough to use rubbers, he's old enough to get shot.

LAMB. Look, we have sanity on our side, and theoretically that should be to our advantage. If we could set up some kind of diversionary tactic ...

GLORIA. (*To Douglas.*) Maybe you could talk to him about sports.

DOUGLAS. Maybe you could let him feel your dry patches.

JIMMY. I know. Let's send out for a pizza.

(*THEY look at him quizzically.*)

JIMMY. I'm kind of hungry myself, and that'll get us to the phone. He looks like a reasonable man; he can understand that there are times when you just gotta have a pizza.

LAMB. That might work. What kind of pizza were you considering? Sicilian or Neapolitan?

JIMMY. I'm not particular. But I like pepperoni.

DOUGLAS. Mushrooms.

GLORIA. Plain for me.

LAMB. (*With a smile.*) I like it plain myself. (*HE approaches Gelardi.*) Mr. Gelardi ... (*GELARDI looks up fiercely.*) I'm sorry if I interrupted you ...

GELARDI. (*Points to Porteus.*) You interrupted *him.*

LAMB. We're going to send out for pizza. Would you like a couple of slices?

GELARDI. Pizza?

LAMB. From Theresa's. They deliver.

GELARDI. I could do some pizza.

DOUGLAS. (*To Sharon and Norma.*) You guys want pizza?

SHARON. What?

DOUGLAS. Just say "yes."

NORMA. Nothing for me. I'm allergic to molds.

ANDREW. I could go for a calzone myself.

LAMB. So how about two pies—one plain, one half-mushroom and half-pepperoni?

GELARDI. (*Points to Mr. Porteus.*) He wants a meatball parmigiana hero.

LAMB. (*Nods.*) I'll just step in the office and call ...

GELARDI. (*Stops him.*) Hold it right there. *I'll* call.

LAMB. (*Masks his disappointment.*) Do you remember the order?

GELARDI. Two pies—one plain, one with mushrooms and pepperoni, half-and-half—and a meatball parmigiana hero.

ANDREW. And a calzone.

LAMB. Do you know the number? 674-5555.

GELARDI. I got it. (*Pause.*) What is it? 647 ...

LAMB. 674-5555. (*GELARDI looks at him blankly.*) Do you want me to write it down?

GELARDI. No, I got it. (*Unsure.*) 6-7-4 ...

GLORIA. It's very simple. Sixty-seven, forty-five, fifty-five, ... five.

GELARDI. (*Bewildered.*) What?

LAMB. Listen, it's 674, and then it's all fives. 5555.

GELARDI. (*Slowly.*) 6-7-4 ... 5 ... 5 ... 5 ...

DOUGLAS. Five! Five!

GELARDI. Five fives?

LAMB. 674-5 ...

GELARDI. 674-5555! I got it! (*Beat.*) It's not easy for

me, all right?

(*GELARDI exits into the office.*
The OTHERS slowly realize that they are now free to make
    their escape. Quietly THEY gather their things and
    start towards the hallway door.
GELARDI suddenly returns.)

  GELARDI. Hold it!

(*THEY freeze in their tracks.*
GELARDI grabs Lamb.)

  GELARDI. You dial. (*To the others.*) And don't get any
ideas about sneaking out. If I count anyone missing,
Chuckles gets it. (*Points the gun at Lamb.*)
  LAMB. (*To the group, nervously.*) Don't do anything
foolish, now.

(*GELARDI and LAMB exit into the office.*)

  GLORIA. At least we're getting something to eat.
  ANDREW. I hope he doesn't forget the calzone.
  DOUGLAS. (*Grabs Andrew.*) Where's that ring, you
son-of-a-bitch?
  ANDREW. I don't have it!

(*DOUGLAS goes through his pockets. HE pulls out vials*
    and packets of assorted drugs, items wrapped in tin-
    foil, and a sandwich bag filled with white powder. HE
    doesn't find the ring.)

ANDREW. See, I'm clean.

DOUGLAS. I know you're hiding it somewhere.

ANDREW. All right, I confess. I stuck it on my dick. Reach right in and take it.

(ANDREW holds his pants open at the waist. DOUGLAS declines the invitation.)

SHARON. *(To Gloria.)* You know, Daddy always did like meatball parmigiana heroes. Spooky, isn't it?

NORMA. But he would have asked for it on a toasted roll.

SHARON. *(Looks at Norma with curiosity.)* How does she know that?

(JIMMY is warmly embracing YOLANDA, who accepts his caresses with a passive tolerance.)

YOLANDA. Do you really think this is the time and the place for this?

JIMMY. I can't help it. I try to let go but my hands stick to your skin like Velcro. You must have Crazy Glue in your pores.

YOLANDA. You're such a poet. You can eat my slice if you want to.

JIMMY. Excuse me?

YOLANDA. My pizza slice. I can't afford to let any greasy foods spoil my complexion. I want to be homecoming queen this fall, and I need to protect this translucent radiance of mine.

(LAMB and GELARDI enter from the office, arguing.)

LAMB. I told you, it was half-mushroom, half pepperoni.

GELARDI. It was half-sausage, half-onions, half-anchovies.

LAMB. That's three halves.

GELARDI. So we make out on the deal. (*To Sharon.*) And a pepper-and-egg hero. Right?

ANDREW. Did you remember the calzone? (*GELARDI snaps his fingers in dismay.*) I knew it.

LAMB. He wouldn't let me talk.

GELARDI. You might have given him a message in code. I'm not stupid, ya know.

DOUGLAS. How are we paying for this? Are we all chipping in?

SHARON. I'm only going to have one slice.

LAMB. My wallet's in the office.

GELARDI. I'm not paying. I have a gun.

DOUGLAS. So on top of everything else, I'm going to get stuck with the bill?

ANDREW. We have some ready cash right here. (*HE starts opening the donation envelopes on the table by the casket.*) Here you go. Ten dollars from Mr. and Mrs. Eugene Gustafson. Lovely people. (*ANDREW opens another card.*) Another ten, from Ellen McDonnell. And it's a Hallmark.

GLORIA. You can't use this money. It belongs to your father. (*SHE opens an envelope herself.*) Two dollars.

DOUGLAS. Two dollars? (*HE takes the card, and reads it.*) Frank McHugh. That cheap prick. (*HE pockets the two dollars.*)

*(The PHONE in the office rings. LAMB starts for the
    office.)*

GELARDI. *(Stops Lamb.)* Wait a minute. *(To Mr.
Porteus.)* Is this some kind of trick?

LAMB. If you let it keep ringing, you'll only raise
suspicions.

*(GELARDI mulls this over a moment, and then darts into
    the office. HE returns with the phone. HE gestures for
    Lamb to answer, while holding the gun close to Lamb's
    head.)*

LAMB. *(Into the phone.)* Good Shepherd Funeral Parlor
... Oh. Yes ... Yes, I got your call ... Well, I plan to pick her
up as soon as possible ... What? He's there *now*? ... Uh—
hold on a minute ... *(Covering the receiver, HE turns to
Gelardi.)* I wonder if you could do me a favor. I have to go
out for a few minutes to pick up a package. I promise you,
I'll be right back.

GELARDI. Where to?

LAMB. Just a few blocks up the street. The Community
Hospital.

GELARDI. The hospital! *(HE breaks into a sweat, and
waves his gun wildly.)*

LAMB. No, no, it has nothing to do with you. I have a
body waiting for me. A little girl. A sweet little girl.
Harmless. Dead, in fact. You might want to talk to her.

GELARDI. I've already got my hands full with this guy.
Don't do me any favors.

LAMB. Well, she's only recently dead; she might not be
in the mood for conversation herself. Please, it's very

important that I leave now. There's a representative from Whiteside's already there, waiting to pounce like a vulture. What do you say?

GELARDI. (*To Mr. Porteus.*) What do *you* say? (*HE listens, and turns gravely.*) He says *no*. Nobody leaves, and that's that.

LAMB. (*Into the phone.*) Listen, I need more time ... You know I'm good for it. Have I ever left you holding the bag? ... But that's not right. I had first dibs ... And they have rats at Whiteside's! Rats! (*HE slams the phone down.*) You'll have to excuse me. I just lost my little girl ... (*HE turns away to hide his tears.*)

GLORIA. (*Prying JIMMY away from YOLANDA.*) You'd better go to your father. He needs you.

(*JIMMY goes over to comfort Lamb.*
ANDREW approaches Gelardi.)

ANDREW. I was in the hospital myself, once. Re-hab. It's not so bad.

GELARDI. It's hell. It's a living death.

ANDREW. But it's for your own good. I was seeing little animals: rabbits, chipmunks ... I was heavily into Disney at the time. But they straightened me out, cleaned me up, and made me face reality. And now I'm a model citizen.

GELARDI. Do you think I'm a menace to society? I'm not anti-social; I have a lot of friends. They just happen not to be alive. Yes, I'm a paranoid schizophrenic, but does that make me a bad person? I don't think so.

ANDREW. Do you need any drugs?

GELARDI. I don't like to do drugs when I'm already

hallucinating.

ANDREW. That's a good rule-of-thumb ...

(JIMMY returns to Yolanda, now that his FATHER has composed himself.)

YOLANDA. Is your father all right?

JIMMY. Yes. He's going through an emotional time.

YOLANDA. Jimmy, there's something very confusing about all this. Your father, for instance: he certainly does make himself at home around here. Answering phones, changing the fuses ... He doesn't act at all like an astrophysicist.

JIMMY. I have something to confess, Yo. I haven't been entirely honest with you.

YOLANDA. What do you mean?

JIMMY. Well ... for one thing, my father is not an astrophysicist.

YOLANDA. He's not?

JIMMY. No. And I'm not a nuclear engineer. I just told you that to impress you.

YOLANDA. *(Shocked.)* You mean you told a lie?

JIMMY. It was only because I found you and your skin so attractive, and I knew that if I told you what I really did ...

YOLANDA. You took advantage of my trusting and ingenuous nature so that you could fondle my skin? How despicable! *(Walking away from him.)* You can't believe anything you hear in bars anymore.

JIMMY. Let me explain ...

YOLANDA. There's nothing to explain. I never want to see you again. And this time I mean it!

(YOLANDA crosses to the other side of the room in a huff. ANDREW and GELARDI share a quiet laugh together, as SHARON observes.)

SHARON. Andrew seems to have found a kindred spirit.

GLORIA. That's what's nice about wakes. You meet people, you make connections. I went to a funeral in Greenpoint—it was my cousin's husband's father—and you know who I met there? Telly Savalas. Before he died. He had his bald head with him and everything.

SHARON. I never cared for him.

GLORIA. Oh, I thought he was sensuous. But that's what wakes are all about: maintaining the social fabric. Besides, it's so nice to have the whole family together again. This is life. What more could you want?

(The DOORBELL rings—a deep, booming, ominous ring.)

DOUGLAS. *(Looking out the window.)* The pizza's here!

(EVERYONE rises in gustatory anticipation.)

BLACKOUT

Scene 2

Morning in the Lilac Room.
There are two pizza cartons, one on a folding chair, one on the floor, both emptied of their contents.

GELARDI is still at the head of the casket, whispering to Mr. Porteus. NORMA is still seated, keeping her vigil. ANDREW is asleep in the armchair. YOLANDA stands by the window, avoiding Jimmy. DOUGLAS is seated, drinking from his flask. SHARON and GLORIA sit together. LAMB sits on the kneeler, his head in his hands. EVERYONE is exhausted and frustrated.
After a moment of silence, SHARON stifles a burp.
THEY all look at her.)

SHARON. Excuse me ... Those onions ...

LAMB. (*Checks his watch.*) The Mass starts in an hour. The pallbearers will be here soon. Really, Mr. Gelardi, you're going to have to make some kind of decision.

(GELARDI pays no attention.
LAMB sits beside Douglas.)

LAMB. It's no use. We'll never make our starting time. In all my years of service, I've never missed a curtain before. When that requiem bell sounded, my casket was *there.* I took pride in that.

DOUGLAS. And rightfully so.

LAMB. And what about Mr. Campbell? He's scheduled for 11:15. The Mayor is supposed to attend. This would have been one of my biggest funerals in years.

DOUGLAS. As we say in my business, "The best-laid plans ... "

LAMB. This is the end for me. If you can't depend on your local mortician, who can you depend on? (*HE takes a swig from Douglas' flask.*)

JIMMY. (*Pining for Yolanda, steals up beside her.*)

Yolanda ...

YOLANDA. (*Shrinks away.*) Please keep your distance.

JIMMY. I can't. I saw the soft down of your cheek glowing in the morning sun, and I felt myself drawn to you, like a moth rushing towards a golden flame ...

YOLANDA. Give it a rest, will you? I've been listening to this crap all night.

JIMMY. If you'd only listen to my heart ...

YOLANDA. You lied to me. I thought I could trust you. I thought you were different.

JIMMY. I am different. I pretended to be a nuclear engineer because I was afraid to tell you what I really do. I was afraid you wouldn't understand.

YOLANDA. How could you think that? I'm a totally understanding person. Doesn't my compassion shine forth like a beacon? It's because I'm so open and vulnerable that I treasure honesty above all virtues. I don't care if you're a dog-catcher, or a garbageman, as long as you're real and forthright, and down-to-earth. Whatever it is, I'll understand.

JIMMY. (*Taking her hands in his own.*) I'm a mortician's apprentice.

YOLANDA. Get your hands off me. (*YOLANDA pushes away from him, shivering.*)

SHARON. (*Regarding Gelardi.*) I wonder what they're talking about? He's got an awfully wild look in his eye.

GLORIA. He really is a handsome man. It's a shame that he's a little unbalanced. You and he would make a nice couple.

SHARON. Are you crazy? There's no future in air-conditioning. (*To Douglas.*) And what's with Norma? She hasn't moved from that chair all night. I still can't figure out what she's doing here.

DOUGLAS. I should think it's pretty obvious: She came to see me.

SHARON. What?

DOUGLAS. You know how hard she took it when I dumped her. Look at the lovesick expression on her face. She's been carrying the torch for twenty years, poor kid. Maybe I should go over and say hello.

SHARON. Yeah, make her day.

GLORIA. (*Grabbing his arm.*) You stay right here. I don't want you talking to her.

DOUGLAS. Don't tell me what to do. Did I say anything when you were shaking your tits at Mr. Personality? (*HE indicates a flustered LAMB. DOUGLAS crosses over to Norma.*) Hi, Norma.

NORMA. Douggie.

DOUGLAS. It's been a long time. I would have come over sooner, but the wife's a little jealous; you know how wives are.

NORMA. Yes, I know.

DOUGLAS. Not that I blame her. The old spark is still there, isn't it? You don't have to say a word—I can see it in your eyes. The Porteus charm leaps across the decades. (*Very discreet.*) Listen, I'm going to be tied up after the burial today—party at the house and all that—but you can reach me at my office anytime ... (*HE hands NORMA his business card.*)

NORMA. (*Reading the card.*) "Douglas Porteus—Condoms are my Bag."

DOUGLAS. Catchy, isn't it?

(*The booming DOORBELL rings.*)

GELARDI. (*Alarmed.*) What's that?

YOLANDA. (*Looking out the window.*) It's a man holding a garbage bag.

GELARDI. (*Rushes to the window.*) I didn't order any garbage. (*To Lamb.*) Who is he?

LAMB. I never saw him before.

GELARDI. (*Ominously.*) There are hairs sticking out of his nose.

(*GELARDI fires his gun through the window, shattering the pane. HE fires three times.*
ANDREW is jolted out of his sleep. HE stands straight up.)

ANDREW. (*Eyes wide.*) Good morning, everyone.

GELARDI. (*Dismayed.*) I missed him. This hasn't been my week.

LAMB. You can't go shooting everyone who comes to my front door. If you shoot the Mayor, I'm telling you right now, I'm going to be very upset.

GELARDI. What's in that bag he dropped? A bomb? A nuclear explosive?

LAMB. I'll be happy to look.

GELARDI. No. (*To Andrew.*) You look. I trust you.

ANDREW. You do?

GELARDI. You're the only one who understands me. (*ANDREW starts towards the door.*) But don't try to escape, or I'll shoot you down like a dog.

ANDREW. I understand. (*ANDREW exits into the hallway.*)

DOUGLAS. (*Turning back to Norma.*) Pretty exciting funeral, huh? So what were we talking about?

NORMA. The burial ... Your father will be buried in the family plot?

DOUGLAS. Yes, we have a section in Holy Rood. Under an apple tree.

NORMA. Is there any extra space?

DOUGLAS. In the limousine?

NORMA. In the grave.

DOUGLAS. Well, I don't know ... It depends on how deep you dig, I suppose ...

NORMA. (*To herself.*) It must be taken care of in the will. He promised.

DOUGLAS. (*Startled.*) The will? Did you say the will?

NORMA. (*Still in a reverie.*) Side by side, through all eternity ...

DOUGLAS. Did Sharon tell you something about the will?

NORMA. Sharon?

DOUGLAS. Yes, Sharon, my darling sister. What did she say to you last night?

NORMA. Oh ... She told me that she had a hard time with your father ... But she knows that she'll get her reward.

DOUGLAS. Her reward?

NORMA. That was the very word she used: reward. She wants to have a life of her own.

DOUGLAS. (*Stares coldly at Sharon.*) I'll just bet she does ...

(*ANDREW appears outside at the window.*)

GELARDI. What is it?

ANDREW. It's a dead dog.

GELARDI. A dead dog? That's a bad omen.

LAMB. Is it a Rottweiler?

ANDREW. It smells pretty bad.

LAMB. You'd better put it downstairs in the freezer.

GELARDI. No, no! No more dead things in the building!

LAMB. It's only a dog. Dogs can't talk.

ANDREW. Except in television shows.

GELARDI. They can bark. They can hound my sleep with their disembodied howls ... What if it's a reincarnated spirit? What if it's possessed by the soul of Hitler?

LAMB. I can't leave a dead dog on my doorstep!

GELARDI. (*Clutching his head.*) Blut! Blut!

LAMB. (*Disgusted, to Gloria.*) I don't know why he has to bring Hitler into this.

GLORIA. Look at the bright side: That poor man he shot at is sure to call the police.

LAMB. True. It's still possible that we can get this situation resolved and start the funeral on schedule. (*To ANDREW, who is climbing through the window.*) Mr. Porteus, would you mind clearing that dog off the front walk? Just throw it in the bushes for now ...

GELARDI. No! No one leaves! (*With mystical fervor.*) The end is near. Soon the dead will walk the earth.

SHARON. Does he mean that Daddy's going to get up out of the casket?

LAMB. Oh, I hope not.

DOUGLAS. What are you afraid of, Sharon? Divine retribution?

SHARON. Pardon me?

DOUGLAS. Your innocence is touching, as always. Have you set a date yet, or will you wait until the inheritance tax is paid?

SHARON. What do you mean?

DOUGLAS. You *are* getting married, aren't you? You're too old to be living in sin.

ANDREW. Who's getting married?

GLORIA. Who's living in sin?

SHARON. I don't know what you're talking about?

DOUGLAS. I'm talking about the will, Miss Executrix. The will.

SHARON. I don't know anything about the will.

DOUGLAS. How long do you expect us to believe that? You and Klenkel have been plotting this all along, with your phone calls and your secret meetings ... tying all the loose ends into a very neat package, I'm sure. Maybe you could fool Andy here, because he's basically an idiot, but I'm a condom salesman, and you can't put one over on me. That will is a fraud, a put-up job right down to the last codicil.

GLORIA. But you haven't even seen the will ...

DOUGLAS. You shut up.

SHARON. Are you suggesting that Larry Klenkel and I changed the will to cheat you out of your measly inheritance?

DOUGLAS. Yes.

SHARON. And that we're involved in some sordid affair?

DOUGLAS. Yes.

SHARON. And that I'm planning to remarry before Daddy is even cold in the grave?

DOUGLAS. Yes, yes, yes!

SHARON. I suppose the next thing you'll say is that the two of us conspired to murder him to get him out of the way!

DOUGLAS. (*Giving this consideration.*) Now that you mention it, he was supposed to die of *cancer* ...

ANDREW. That's right.

SHARON. He died of a heart attack. He was a sick man, and sick men die of heart attacks.

DOUGLAS. So do poisoned men. (*To Lamb.*) Isn't that so?

LAMB. That's not my area of expertise. I'm concerned with effect, not cause.

SHARON. I wasn't even with him when he died.

DOUGLAS. And where were you? At the Meadowbrook Motel, testing out the waterbeds?

SHARON. We don't go to motels! (*SHE stops short.*)

ANDREW. (*With quiet admiration.*) Trapped into a damaging admission.

DOUGLAS. (*With great relish.*) So now the truth comes out. And where do your pathetic little party games take place?

SHARON. I don't have to answer to you. I've gone through hell the last two years, and now I have a chance to live my own life, and find some small measure of happiness with a wonderful man, and I'm going to go for it. And if you don't like it, you can just go fuck yourself. (*A parting shot.*) And furthermore, Larry won't even use your condoms. He says they're *porous*.

DOUGLAS. There's no need to get nasty. I'm not one to dwell on the past—if you killed Dad, that's your business. But that bogus will won't stand up in court and you know it. Therefore, as the first-born, I have no other choice but to invoke the ancient right of primogeniture, and assume control of the general estate. We'll see who winds up fucking whom's self.

ANDREW. Bear with me a moment, because I'm basically an idiot, but what do you mean by "the general estate"?

DOUGLAS. The house, the furniture, the property, the bank accounts, the stocks ... and, of course, the empty lot on Elm Avenue.

ANDREW. That doesn't leave an awful lot for me, does it?

DOUGLAS. As if you deserved a dime after the way you disappointed the old man and broke his heart—always stoned, dropping out of college, no jobs, no prospects ... you're a total screw-up, and that's all you'll ever be.

ANDREW. Consistency is a reliable yardstick of success.

DOUGLAS. Whereas I am a respected businessman, a pillar of the community, and the only one in this family who's done anything worthwhile with his life. I have a moral right to that money. (*To Lamb*.) First-born takes all—correct me if I'm wrong.

LAMB. Well, it doesn't seem exactly fair.

DOUGLAS. Fair? Who cares about fair? Do you worry about fair when a little girl gets hit by a bus?

LAMB. Let's not get melodramatic. It was only a car.

DOUGLAS. Money goes to money; *that's* fair. Besides, I was always Dad's favorite. He thought the world of me.

SHARON. He thought you were an asshole!

ANDREW. Everybody thinks you're an asshole. I keep trying to tell you that.

SHARON. Who's been taking care of the goddamn house since Ma died? I have! I did more for Daddy in one week than either of you did in a year.

ANDREW. But I was in jail.

DOUGLAS. I don't wish to belabor the point, but as the first-born ...

SHARON. You're only first-born because you were born first. I'm a divorced woman trying to make ends meet in a man's world. I need that money.

ANDREW. What about me? I'm a total screw-up, I'm a charity case, and I want that dining-room clock!

SHARON. *I* want the clock!

DOUGLAS. I'm the first-born!

ANDREW. I'm the last-born!

SHARON. I emptied his bed-pans!

NORMA. (*Suddenly rising from her chair.*) I'm carrying his child!

(A stunned silence follows this revelation.)

ANDREW. Can anyone top that?

SHARON. (*Approaching Norma cautiously.*) Norma, dear, do you want to lie down?

NORMA. There's nothing wrong with me. I'm carrying his child. I thought you might like to know.

DOUGLAS. The heat's getting to her.

GLORIA. She looks a little bloated, but I thought that was her natural fat.

ANDREW. (*To Douglas.*) Maybe she means she's carrying *your* kid.

GLORIA. What?

NORMA. I'm carrying Walter's child. We've been lovers for some time. (*Beat.*) I hope this hasn't come as a shock to anyone.

SHARON. Norma, are you sure you're at the right

wake? This is my father's wake. He was seventy-two years old. This is him, right here. This old man.

NORMA. He was old, but he had a young heart.

DOUGLAS. If he had such a young heart, why did it happen to stop on him?

NORMA. He always tried so hard ... He was intent on giving pleasure to others. His death was a happy one.

(The FAMILY MEMBERS exchange amazed glances.)

LAMB. (*Appalled.*) Good Lord.

DOUGLAS. Are you trying to tell us that ... you were *there*, when ... when ... ?

NORMA. (*Nods.*) His last word was "Yes ... !"

ANDREW. Well, he went out on a positive note.

GLORIA. I wonder what the question was?

SHARON. (*Bridling.*) I don't believe a word of it. You haven't been near our house in twenty years.

NORMA. Walter wanted to keep it a secret, for obvious reasons. It started back in high school. At your sweet-sixteen party, in fact. The first time I saw your father sitting in his easy chair, wearing his cardigan sweater, with the heady scent of Vitalis in his hair, I knew that I had found a sympathetic soul.

DOUGLAS. But that was before we started going out.

NORMA. I'm afraid I used you, Douggie, to be close to your father. It was a dirty trick, but it was for the sake of love.

DOUGLAS. Now you're being absurd. Everyone knows you were crazy about me.

NORMA. Actually I always thought you were sort of ... (*SHE leaves the thought unfinished.*)

ANDREW. An asshole?
DOUGLAS. Shut up.

(HE takes NORMA aside.)

DOUGLAS. How can you say that? We were a perfect couple. You were hopelessly in love with me.
NORMA. I never loved you, Douggie.
DOUGLAS. Of course you loved me. You just don't remember. Why, I did things with you that I've never even done with my own wife.
NORMA. Superficial gratification, nothing more. My body was with you, but my heart was with Walter. No other man has satisfied me so completely. When I think of the countless hours we spent together in his little bedroom at the top of the stairs, hours of pleasure, hours of ecstasy ...
SHARON. It's impossible. I was there every day.
NORMA. Yes, and it was very kind of you to change the sheets.
SHARON. This is all fantasy, the product of a sick, unbalanced mind ...
NORMA. *(Takes a key from her purse.)* Nevertheless, you will recognize your father's house key.

(SHARON inspects the key with dismay.)

NORMA. Walter had always planned to carry our secret to his grave. But now that the grave is so near, and the terms of the final will are shortly to be disclosed, I see no reason to maintain my silence.
DOUGLAS. *(With foreboding.)* The final will?
NORMA. The Last Will and Testament, which of course

voids all previous wills.

SHARON. Now I know you're lying. Larry has the will in his office safe, and it hasn't been changed in three years.

NORMA. Walter didn't deposit the new will with Mr. Klenkel. He thought it more prudent to go to a disinterested third party. Someone who wasn't sleeping with his daughter.

SHARON. (*Shaken by this disclosure.*) How did he find out?

NORMA. I may have mentioned it to him. I try to keep tabs on everyone in the family. Who's doing what, to whom, and where.

(THEY are all uneasy with this thought.)

NORMA. I have to protect the interests of my child.

DOUGLAS. And what does the Last Will say?

NORMA. I don't know all the details. I'm sure you're all provided for, in some measure. (*Beat.*) But the house is mine. It has a nice big backyard, for your little brother to play in.

DOUGLAS. We can contest that will easily enough.

NORMA. (*Pats her midsection.*) You can't contest *this*, honey. By the time you get anything in court I'll have Rambo Junior squalling in my arms, a most persuasive piece of evidence.

GLORIA. Rambo, Junior?

DOUGLAS. (*Points to Mr. Porteus.*) Are we to assume that this is Rambo, Senior?

NORMA. We had pet names for each other. I called him Rambo—what else could you call him?—and he called me Princess.

SHARON. (*Outraged.*) Princess! (*SHE rushes over to the casket.*) Is it true? You called that slut "Princess"?

GELARDI. Hey, back off. He only talks to me.

SHARON. Then ask him who took care of him all these years, who cut up his meat and wiped his chin and his nose and anything else that had to be wiped! Who gave tirelessly of her time and energy, without a word of complaint or a thought for herself! Me, that's who! Me! Not that phony Polish porkbutt! (*To Mr. Porteus.*) I was your Princess, you ungrateful old bastard, me, little Sharon, little Princess Sharon ... ! (*SHE falls to her knees, slumps against the casket, sobbing.*)

GELARDI. Are there any other questions?

ANDREW. Ask him what the story is with this babe. Has he really been boffing her for the past twenty years?

DOUGLAS. And was she with him when he died? Maybe we can nail her for manslaughter.

NORMA. (*To Gelardi.*) Tell him I'll always love him, and cherish his memory ...

DOUGLAS. Don't prejudice the witness.

GLORIA. What does he say about the will?

ANDREW. Did I get the clock?

DOUGLAS. If I'm not in that will, I'm boycotting this funeral. Tell him that.

NORMA. He never liked you, anyway.

DOUGLAS. (*Raises his arm threateningly.*) If you weren't pregnant ...

LAMB. (*Breaking this up.*) Please, please! This behavior is unacceptable! I will not stand by while you presume to interrogate a corpse!

DOUGLAS. If my Dad is speaking from beyond the grave, I want to hear what he has to say.

ANDREW. (*Notices that GELARDI has his ear cocked to the casket.*) Shh ... We're getting an audio feed.

(*ALL gather at the casket expectantly.*)

DOUGLAS. Well?
GELARDI. He says the tombs will open and disgorge, the earth yield up a rotting harvest, all the dead will parade in a festival of decay. Death, death is on the march ... !
DOUGLAS. (*Angrily.*) What about the *will*?
NORMA. The dead often speak in riddles.
DOUGLAS. Riddles, my ass. This is a lot of horseshit. (*To Gelardi.*) I was willing to give you the benefit of the doubt before, but it's time you came up with some real answers. We don't want to hear about zombies marching down Main Street. We want to hear about our money!
GLORIA. Don't get excited ...
DOUGLAS. I *will* get excited. I've just about had enough. I've been held at gunpoint for the last twelve hours, I'm hot, I'm hungry, I'm surrounded by my nitwit relatives, you're trying to pick up the undertaker, and this bimbo is telling me that I'm going to have a new brother, which I need like a hole in the head. And now I can't even get a straight answer out of my own dead father! The whole thing is just pissing me off. (*DOUGLAS sits down, fuming.*)
GELARDI. What's his problem?
GLORIA. He's always this way in the morning.
GELARDI. The next time he yells at me like that, I'm going to shoot him. And that goes for the rest of you. Why don't you all sit down? Get away from me! (*As THEY back away.*) I give them a message from the dead, and they still

complain. Some people are never satisfied.

GLORIA. (*Helps SHARON to her feet.*) Come on, Princess. (*SHE guides SHARON to a seat, and warns Douglas.*) He's going to shoot you if you don't behave.

(*DOUGLAS waves disdainfully.*
LAMB sits down next to Jimmy.)

LAMB. Jimmy, I want you to do me a favor. If I don't get out of this alive, I want you to have me cremated.

JIMMY. Cremated?

LAMB. Somehow the thought of being casketed has lost all its charm for me.

JIMMY. I can't believe it. Ever since I was a kid you've been telling me all about your dream funeral.

LAMB. It seems so self-indulgent now. Just incinerate me, and leave me to the mercy of the winds.

JIMMY. You need some sleep.

LAMB. An eternity's worth. I don't want you to worry about my will. Your inheritance is secure. I don't have any surprise mistresses—(*Glances at Gloria.*) Not at the moment, anyway—and I have no qualms about leaving the business in your capable hands.

JIMMY. Dad ... (*Glances at Yolanda.*) I'm not taking over the business.

LAMB. What?

JIMMY. I don't want to be a mortician.

LAMB. Don't want to be a mortician ... ? Can you be serious?

JIMMY. I don't think it's right for me. I don't have a feel for the work.

LAMB. That's not so. You have the makings of a great

mortician. You have soul. Listen to me, Jimmy, this place is a gold mine. People always have to die.

JIMMY. I've sort of made up my mind. Maybe this wasn't the best time to tell you ...

LAMB. Who's putting you up to this? Your albino friend?

JIMMY. She has nothing to do with it ...

LAMB. Let me tell you something: She may promote the illusion of dermal perfection, but the next time she steps out of a shower you might take note of that mole on her left cheek.

JIMMY. Mole?

LAMB. Yes, with a few silken tendrils protruding. Not to mention an ongoing battle with acne. Oh, she covers her tracks well, but I have a trained eye. I'd like to see her in a bathing suit; I'd lay even money there's silicone in them thar hills ...

JIMMY. (*Angrily.*) That's enough. I won't have you impugning Yolanda's complexion!

LAMB. Jimmy ... Don't make any rash decisions. I'm sorry if I gave offense, but this comes as a grave disappointment to me. I'd always assumed that, when it came time for me to go, you would be there to take care of me. How can you walk away from all this?

JIMMY. If you must know, Dad ... I don't like dead people.

(LAMB is stunned.)

SHARON. I still can't get over it. My own father, screwed to death by Norma Czerniawski.

DOUGLAS. That baby is the real fly in the ointment. If

only he'd used a Porteus Portable ...

NORMA. (*Turns to Andrew, sitting beside her.*) Andy, I realize that everyone will think my motives were selfish and materialistic, and that I'm nothing more than a scheming golddigger. But I want you to know that I truly loved your father, and no man can ever take his place in my heart.

ANDREW. Will you marry me?

NORMA. (*Startled.*) Why would I want to marry you?

ANDREW. Well, it would really burn Douggie's ass if I wound up with the house. It's something to think about.

LAMB. (*Stands by the casket, talking to Gelardi.*) ... You work and slave to give your kids a better chance in the world, and they throw it back in your face. Doesn't like dead people ... ! (*HE shakes his head in disbelief.*)

GELARDI. He's young.

LAMB. Someday we'll all be too good to bury our dead, and then what? Doesn't Mr. Porteus have his rights, too? He's passing through for the last time, and he wants to look his best. It was up to me to crystallize his essence— what he is, what he was, what he will remain in the gossamer web of memory—and I think I did a damn good job. He's not complaining, is he?

GELARDI. No, he speaks very highly of you.

LAMB. Because I'm a craftsman. Each man is a separate work of art, and I'm like the critic who discovers him, the technician who restores him, the curator who sets him like a pearl in the context of his ... (*LAMB stops short. HE reaches into the casket and lifts out the chewed crust of a pizza slice. HE tries to contain his fury.*) Who threw the pizza crust in Mr. Porteus' casket? (*No one responds.*) Well, that's the last straw. I've tolerated a host of abominations from you people, but now I've had it! It isn't enough that you exhibit the most offensive manners in the presence of the Beloved, but now, finally, to use his casket, the receptacle of his cherished remains, as a garbage can ... ! It is unspeakable! (*Struggles to regain his composure.*) You're all the same, aren't you? You parade in here in all your finery, you shed a few respectable tears, and tomorrow you're back living your lives and the whole ugly business is forgotten. But keep in mind, you're all going to die someday—yes, even you, Miss Kamola, with your phosphorescent skin—you're all going to take your turn on the bier, and perhaps you'll be attended in your repose by a horde of stupid, inconsiderate parasites who share your contempt for the sanctity of the solemn rites. Perhaps you'll be buried in a pile of pizza crusts. Would you like that? Would you? (*Approaching the casket.*) This is a corpse. And a corpse has his own innate dignity. When you stand before him squabbling about your trivial problems. you commit an offense against his nature. Fighting, belching, farting, discussing your various intimate couplings ... all of which I would find distasteful even under ordinary circumstances, but here, in the House of Death ... ! (*Sighing.*) Maybe I'm wrong. Maybe I'm being too subjective. My wife could never understand ... "Why do you have to spend so much time at the mortuary? Why can't you play golf on Sundays, like everyone else?" Because this is my calling! Yes, there's formaldehyde on my hands, and I'm damned proud of it! What greater gift can a man possess, than the ability to serve all men, both the living and the dead? To feel a kinship with past generations, to secure a place in the continuity of time? Other men fear Death, out of ignorance, but I welcome him like a benevolent uncle. Uncle Death ... See how well he sits with Mr. Porteus. Here is peace. Here is placid serenity. The soul has taken wing, and the body silently rejoices. When I stand here and observe the daily miracle of mortality, my bosom swells with pride, and I can declare with moral fervor and surety of purpose, "Yes! I am a mortician!" (*With contempt.*) But what do you care? You're too busy grabbing for money, grabbing for drugs, grabbing for sex ... You make me sick! You don't deserve a decent funeral! I hope you all die in a plane crash, and they have to pick you up with a shovel, and you get buried with someone else's body parts. Insensitive swine! (*LAMB has nothing more to say. HE turns away.*)

(*A pause.*)

ANDREW. Uncle Death?
GLORIA. I don't remember anyone farting.

(*A POLICE SIREN wails offstage.*)

GELARDI. (*Rushes to the window.*) The police! I'm cornered! Trapped like a rat! They'll take me back to that hospital! They'll tie me up, and stick wires in my head, and electrify my brain!
ANDREW. Some of those nurses are hot, though.
GELARDI. I have to escape! (*HE looks at the coffin.*) Wait a minute ... This will do nicely. (*GELARDI sweeps the floral blanket off the coffin and lifts the bottom lid.*)
LAMB. What are you doing?
GELARDI. (*Brandishing the gun.*) I'm borrowing the coffin. You don't mind, do you? (*To Andrew.*) Give me a

hand here. (*HE grabs Mr. Porteus.*)

SHARON. Stop that! Didn't you hear what he just said about respect for the dead?

GELARDI. Your father says it's perfectly all right. He doesn't need the casket, anyway. He's going to be marching soon, marching, marching ...

LAMB. Be careful now, don't rip any of the stitches ...

DOUGLAS. (*Rebuffing Lamb.*) You keep your hands off him. He's our father, we can handle him. (*Pushing Gelardi out of the way.*) Excuse me.

(*DOUGLAS takes the head, while ANDREW goes to the feet. With a grunt, DOUGLAS and ANDREW lift Mr. Porteus out of the coffin and carry him to the armchair.*)

ANDREW. I thought he'd be lighter.

(*THEY rest Mr. Porteus in the armchair, sitting up. SHARON tries to arrange his hands, which are tangled in the rosary beads. NORMA fusses with his hair. In the meantime GELARDI climbs into the casket.*)

GELARDI. This is the plan. You carry me out to the hearse, and drive it down the block. You can let me out around the corner.

SHARON. (*Notices the Celtic ring on Norma's finger. Grabbing NORMA's hand.*) Where did you get that ring?

ANDREW. (*Stepping up.*) From me. It's an engagement ring.

DOUGLAS. What?

SHARON. You mean ... ?

NORMA. I know it seems sudden, but I do want my son to be a legitimate Porteus.

GLORIA. But that would make Andrew his own brother's father.

ANDREW. And there's not too many men who can say that.

GELARDI. (*Impatiently.*) I hope I'm not rushing you people! I want the women in front, in case they open fire. The pregnant one goes first. Let's go, line up.

DOUGLAS. Listen, before we go, could you do me a favor, and maybe shoot a few people? Norma over there, and possibly my brother?

ANDREW. (*Back at Douglas.*) He's the one you should be shooting.

LAMB. Why don't you shoot them all? I could use the business.

SHARON. You're crazy if you think we'd let you bury us.

GELARDI. I can't shoot anybody now, with the police surrounding us. If you wanted somebody shot, you should have said something earlier. Are we all set? (*GELARDI lays back in the coffin.*) This is really comfortable, you know?

LAMB. (*Lowering the casket lid.*) Watch your fingers.

GELARDI. (*As the lid closes.*) I wish they had lights in this thing ...

LAMB. Jimmy, give me a hand here.

DOUGLAS. (*To Lamb.*) We don't need any help from you.

(*DOUGLAS and ANDREW start wheeling the casket. GLORIA drifts back to Lamb.*)

GLORIA. I just want you to know that you can bury me anytime.

LAMB. I appreciate that.

DOUGLAS. Gloria! Get back in line.

(GLORIA joins SHARON and NORMA in front of the casket.

As THEY lead the way, DOUGLAS and ANDREW roll the casket out through the doors. LAMB follows them.)

LAMB. Don't trip over the dog.

(THEY exit.)

YOLANDA. Are they really going to help him escape?

JIMMY. (*Looking out the window.*) No, they're loading him into the police van.

YOLANDA. You can't trust anyone anymore.

JIMMY. You can trust me.

YOLANDA. It's no use, Jimmy. I can never think of you in the same way. I'll always see you standing in a grave; and that particular image just doesn't do anything for me.

JIMMY. But that's all over with. I'm going to be a normal person, and do normal things. I'll be a dogcatcher, or a garbageman, and I'll make you proud of me.

YOLANDA. It's too late. Can't you see? It's a question of personal integrity. I'm so pure, and fine, and good. How can I spend my life in the shadow of death? It's inappropriate.

JIMMY. (*Bitterly.*) You're not all that pure.

YOLANDA. Purity is a matter of appearance. I happen

to possess a certain luminosity, an almost saintly incandescence. It's a carefully nurtured image, and I have to protect it at all costs.

JIMMY. I don't see what's so incandescent about a few shots of silicone.

YOLANDA. Pardon me?

JIMMY. And what about your luminous acne condition?

YOLANDA. (*Uneasily.*) That's not funny. I get very nervous just thinking about acne.

JIMMY. I guess you have enough trouble trying to cover that mole.

YOLANDA. Mole?

JIMMY. The mole on your cheek!

YOLANDA. (*Claps her hand to her cheek in horror.*) How can you see it?

JIMMY. I have a trained eye. It's quite repulsive, isn't it?

YOLANDA. (*Inspects her face with a cosmetic mirror.*) This fucking humidity, it's eroding my base ... !

JIMMY. The mole itself isn't so bad, but those stringy hairs ... What, do you paste them down?

YOLANDA. How can you be so cruel?

JIMMY. I see flesh rot every day. It's no big deal.

YOLANDA. (*Rushing from him.*) I never want to see you again ... !

JIMMY. Go on, get out of here, and take your unsightly blemishes with you!

(*YOLANDA flees from the room, just as LAMB is re-entering.*)

LAMB. (*Pointing helpfully down the hall.*) Second door

to your left.

(YOLANDA exits.
The SIREN wails offstage.
LAMB watches from the window.)

LAMB. So much for that. We'll have to pick out a new casket for Mr. Porteus ... That is, if you don't mind soiling your hands with this dirty business.
JIMMY. Dad ... I was thinking about what you said. And maybe I was too hasty.
LAMB. You mean ... You might reconsider ... ?
JIMMY. I see things a lot clearer now. And I've learned something from this experience.
LAMB. What have you learned?
JIMMY. Well ... I've learned that human beings are strange creatures: petty, vicious, self-centered, stupid ... But once they're dead, they're all right.
LAMB. (*Beaming.*) My son!

(LAMB puts his arm around Jimmy, and with renewed
purpose THEY walk out of the Lilac Room.
MR. PORTEUS remains seated.)

THE END

COSTUME PLOT

MARTIN LAMB: Dark suit and tie. Flower in lapel.

JIMMY LAMB: Dark suit and tie—identical to his father.

SHARON MULDOON: Dark grey dress. Heels.

DOUGLAS PORTEUS: Dark suit.

ANDREW PORTEUS: Blazer and slacks, unmatched and wrinkled.

GLORIA PORTEUS: Tight one-piece dress, low-cut. High heels.

BOBBY GELARDI: Orange jumpsuit, with lettering: "Bobby." Work boots.

NORMA CZERNIAWSKI: Black dress, wide black hat with veil. Heels.

YOLANDA KAMOLA: Yellow summer dress, floral print. White shoes.

PROPERTY PLOT

ONSTAGE PROPS

Memorial cards
Mass cards
Register book
Pen with chain
Floral blanket on casket
Toy fire truck (inside casket)
Electric fan
Rosary
Pizza Cartons (2) Pizza crust (inside casket)
Statue of saint (breakaway)

OFFSTAGE PROPS

In Office: Telephone. Air fresheners. Candles. Flashlight.

INDIVIDUAL PROPS

LAMB: Notebook. Pen. Handkerchief.
JIMMY : Chamois cloth
SHARON: Handkerchief. Handbag.
DOUGLAS: Condom packets. Flask.
ANDREW: Drug paraphernalia. Razor blade. Celtic ring.
GELARDI: Toolbox. Gun.
NORMA: Key ring.
YOLANDA: Handbag. Cosmetic mirror.

SOUND PLOT

Pre-show Music: appropriately solemn (e.g. Funeral
March from Mahler's First Symphony)
Muzak (Act I, Sc. 1)
Telephone (Act 1, Sc. 1)
Telephone (Act I, Sc. 2)
Telephone (Act II, Sc. 1)
Doorbell (Act II, sc. 1)
Doorbell (Act II, Sc. 2)
Police siren (Act II, Sc. 2)

A GOOD MAN

GROUND PLOT

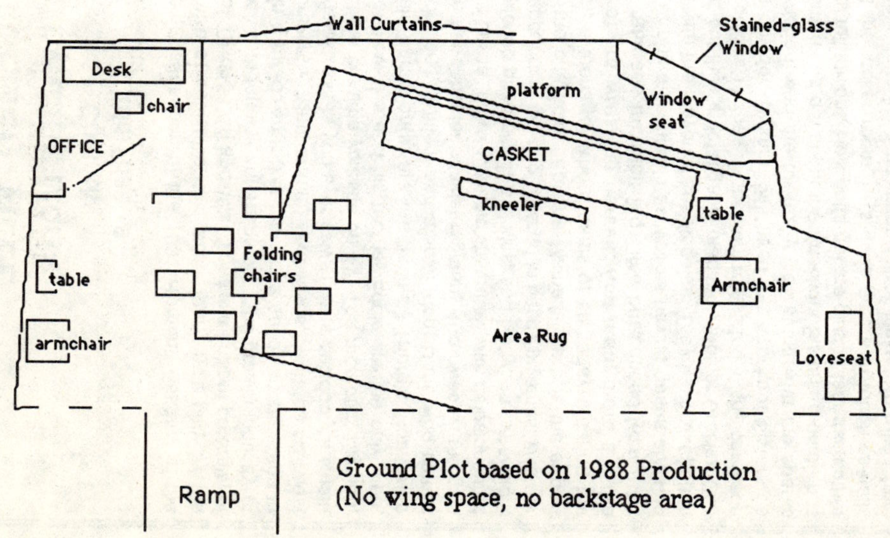

Ground Plot based on 1988 Production
(No wing space, no backstage area)

CEMENTVILLE
by Jane Martin
Comedy
Little Theatre

(5m., 9f.) Int. The comic sensation of the 1991 Humana Festival at the famed Actors Theatre of Louisville, this wildly funny new play by the mysterious author of *Talking With* and *Vital Signs* is a brilliant portrayal of America's fascination with fantasy entertainment, "the growth industry of the 90's." We are in a run-down locker room in a seedy sports arena in the Armpit of the Universe, "Cementville, Tennessee," with the scurviest bunch of professional wrasslers you ever saw. This is decidedly a small-time operation—not the big time you see on TV. The promoter, Bigman, also appears in the show. He and his brother Eddie are the only men, though; for the main attraction(s) are the "ladies." There's Tiger, who comes with a big drinking problem and a small dog; Dani, who comes with a large chip on her shoulder against Bigman, who owes all the girls several weeks' pay; Lessa, an ex-Olympic shotputter with delusions that she is actually employed presently in athletics; and Netty, an overweight older woman who appears in the ring dressed in baggy pajamas, with her hair in curlers, as the character "Pajama Mama." There is the eager-beaver go-fer Nola, a teenager who dreams of someday entering the glamorous world of pro wrestling herself. And then, there are the Knockout Sisters, refugees from the Big Time but banned from it for heavy-duty abuse of pharmaceuticals as well as having gotten arrested *in flagrante delicto* with the Mayor of Los Angeles. They have just gotten out of the slammer; but their indefatigable manager, Mother Crocker ("Of the Auto-Repair Crockers") hopes to get them reinstated, if she can keep them off the white powder. Bigman has hired the Knockout Sisters as tonight's main attraction, and the fur really flies along with the sparks when the other women find out about the Knockout Sisters. Bigman has really got his hands full tonight. He's gotta get the girls to tear each other up in the ring, not the locker room; he's gotta deal with tough-as-nails Mother Crocker; he's gotta keep an arena full of tanked-up rubes from tearing up the joint—and he's gotta solve the mystery of who bit off his brother Eddie's dick last night. (#5580)

TWO NEW COMEDIES FROM
SAMUEL FRENCH, Inc.

FAST GIRLS. **(Little Theatre). Comedy.** Diana Amsterdam. 2m., 3f. Int. Lucy Lewis is a contemporary, single woman in her thirties with what used to be called a "healthy sex life," much to the chagrin of her mother, who feels Lucy is too fast, too easy—and too single. Her best friend, on the other hand, neighbor Abigail McBride, is deeply envious of Lucy's ease with men. When Lucy wants to date a man she just calls him up, whereas Abigail sits home alone waiting for Ernest, who may not even know she exists, to call. The only time Abigail isn't by the phone is after Lucy has had a hot date, when she comes over to Lucy's apartment to hear the juicy details and get green with envy. Sometimes, though, Lucy doesn't want to talk about it, which drives Abigail *nuts* ("If you don't tell me about men I have no love life!"). Lucy's mother arrives to take the bull by the horns, so to speak, arriving with a challenge. Mom claims no man will marry Lucy (even were she to *want to* get married), because she's too easy. Lucy takes up the challenge, announcing that she is going to get stalwart ex-boyfriend Sidney ("we're just friends") Epstein to propose to her. Easier said than done. Sidney doesn't *want* a fast girl. Maybe dear old Mom is right, thinks Lucy. Maybe fast girls *can't* have it all. "Amsterdam makes us laugh, listen and think."—Daily Record. "Brilliantly comic moments."—The Monitor. "rapidly paced comedy with a load of laughs . . . a funny entertainment with some pause for reflection on today's [sexual] confusion."—Suburban News. "Takes a penetrating look at [contemporary sexual chaos]. Passion, celibacy, marriage, fidelity are just some of the subjects that Diana Amsterdam hilariously examines."—Tribune News. (#8149)

ADVICE FROM A CATERPILLAR. **(Little Theatre.) Comedy.** Douglas Carter Beane. 2m. 2f. 1 Unit set & 1 Int. Ally Sheedy and Dennis Christopher starred in the delightful off-Broadway production of this hip new comedy. Ms. Sheedy played Missy, an avant garde video artist who specializes in re-runs of her family's home videos, adding her own disparaging remarks. Needless to say, she is very alienated from the middle-class, family values she grew up with, which makes her very *au courant*, but strangely unhappy. She has a successful career and a satisfactory love-life with a businessman named Suit. Suit's married, but that doesn't stop him and Missy from carrying on. Something's missing, though—and Missy isn't sure what it is, until she meets Brat. He is a handsome young aspiring actor. Unfortunately, Brat is also the boyfriend of Missy's best friend. Sound familiar? It isn't—because Missy's best friend is a gay man named Spaz! Spaz has been urging Missy to find an unmarried boyfriend, but this is too much—too much for Spaz, too much for Suit and, possibly, too much for Missy. Does she *want* a serious relationship (ugh—how bourgeois!)? Can a bisexual unemployed actor actually be her Mr. Wonderful? "Very funny ... a delightful evening."—Town & Village. (#3876)

Other Publications for Your Interest

LLOYD'S PRAYER
(LITTLE THEATRE—COMEDY)
By KEVIN KLING

3 men, 1 woman (1 man & 1 woman play various parts). Bare stage w/set pieces.

Be amazed! The author of the amazing *21A* has fashioned a hilarious comic parable about Bob, the Raccoon Boy, and what happens to him when he is "rescued" from the raccoons who raised him and taught what it means to be human. At first, Bob can only make whirring raccoon sounds, but he is taught to speak by a delightfully whacko "Mom and Dad". He is taken from his cage at Mom and Dad's house by an ambitious ex-con named Lloyd, who sees the raccoon boy as his ticket to fame and fortune. When his first idea— displaying Bob as a carny sideshow freak—fails, Lloyd gets the brilliant idea to become a religious evangelist, displaying Bob as another sort of freak: a miracle from God. Lloyd's pitch, a promise of inspiration "that will bring grown men to a sitting position and women to a greater understanding of themselves", makes them both celebrities. By this time, Bob speaks pretty well ("I've been called many things in my life...But I prefer 'Bob'"), and is on the verge of innocence corrupted when there appears on the scene a beautiful guardian angel, dressed as a high school cheerleader. "Be amazed!", she declares, admonishing Bob to beware of Lloyd. What ensues is an amusing tug-of-war between the angel and Lloyd, with Bob the Raccoon Boy as the rope. The unqualified hit of the Actors Theatre of Louisville 1988 Humana Festival, this brilliant new comedy is "a whirlwind of original humor that comes in waves."—Lexington Herald-Leader. "Fresh, funny and charming."— Columbus Dispatch. "Kling is quite simply a comic genius."—Dramatics Magazine.

(#13997)

21A
(ADVANCED GROUPS—COMEDY)
By KEVIN KLING

1 man—Bare stage w/chairs.

"Astonishing", was the way Newsweek Magazine summed up this one-man tour-de-force in which Mr. Kling performed all the riders on a Minneapolis city bus: eight characters, including the driver. Structured as a series of monologues which in "real life" are going on simultaneously, this hilarious and decidedly "different" play had them rolling in the aisles at Louisville's famed Humana Festival where it won the prestigious Heideman Award. Kling started with the droll driver and moved on to such odd-balls as Gladys, Chairman Francis (a religious proselytizer), Captain Twelve-Pack (a drunk with a beer 12-pack box over his head) and a businessman who is decidedly *not* "Dave", no matter how fervently Captain Twelve-Pack insists that he *is*. And: who is the mysterious intruder sitting at the back of the bus? "Stunning."—U.S.A. Today.

(#22237)